CHRISTIAN DIETRICH GRABBE

by

Roy C. Cowen

Christian Dietrich Grabbe (1801-1836), known by his contemporaries and immediate successors less by his works than by his personality, bore all the characteristics usually associated with erratic genius. Because his dramas revealed the same qualities and were correspondingly revolutionary, his age did not accord them their just recognition but only considered them curiosities. With the advent of Naturalism in the 1880's, however, critics like Karl Bleibtreu suddenly ranked him above even Kleist and Hebbel. Although such praise was based on an excess of enthusiasm, it soon became apparent that Grabbe would never again slip into obscurity. Wedekind, the Expressionists, Brecht and the Absurdists were yet to draw heavily on his exploratory efforts, which anticipated their own "modern" techniques and ideas.

Although Grabbe did not live long enough to realize his full potential, he nevertheless created a series of dramas distinct from each other in subject, technique and form. The present study, while primarily concerned with introducing this pioneer of modern drama to an audience largely unfamiliar with most of his diverse production, also shows those unifying themes and characters that not only characterize his individual position in German literature but also link him with such *Weltschmerzler* as Büchner,

TWAYNE'S WORLD AUTHORS SERIES (TWAS)

The purpose of TWAS is to survey the major writers —novelists, dramatists, historians, poets, philosophers, and critics—of the nations of the world. Among the national literatures covered are those of Australia, Canada, China, Eastern Europe, France, Germany, Greece, India, Italy, Japan, Latin America, New Zealand, Poland, Russia, Scandinavia, Spain, and the African nations, as well as Hebrew, Yiddish, and Latin Classical literatures. This survey is complemented by Twayne's United States Authors Series and English Authors Series.

The intent of each volume in these series is to present a critical-analytical study of the works of the writer; to include biographical and historical material that may be necessary for understanding, appreciation, and critical appraisal of the writer; and to present all material in clear, concise English—but not to vitiate the scholarly content of the work by doing so.

Christian Dietrich Grabbe

By ROY C. COWEN
University of Michigan

Heine and Lenau, in other words, with the general reaction against the idealism of Goethe, Schiller and the Romantics as well as against the saccharine *Biedermeier* literature of the times.

ABOUT THE AUTHOR

Roy C. Cowen is Professor of German at the University of Michigan, where he has taught since 1960. He received his B.A. from Yale University and Dr. phil. from the University of Göttingen. Besides editing plays by Grabbe, Büchner and Grillparzer, he has published an extensive bibliography of nineteenth century German literature. He has also contributed articles on Lessing, Grillparzer, Grabbe, Büchner, Keller, and Goering to various American and European periodicals. Currently he is completing a book on German Naturalism and a two-volume edition of Grabbe's works, both for publication in Germany.

New York

To Hildegard

CHRISTIAN DIETRICH GRABBE

Preface

The present book is intended primarily as an introduction for English speakers to Christian Dietrich Grabbe's life, his works, and his significance in German literary history. Assuming that most readers have read few, if any, of Grabbe's works, I have provided rather detailed plot summaries. It is, nevertheless, my hope that the interpretations and particularly the emphasis on recurring themes and forms will contribute to a more consistent and unified image of Grabbe's dramas than is generally presented in the critical literature on them.

The limits of the present study did not allow a separate chapter on the Grabbe research of recent years, which has considerably grown and should be reviewed. I have, however, tried to indicate, as far as possible, some of the more salient contributions made by individual scholars. An extensive, though selective, bibliography is appended.

All translations are my own. Page references for quotations from Grabbe's works are to the critical edition, *Christian Dietrich Grabbe: Werke*, ed. Alfred Bergmann (Emsdetten: Lechte, 1960-ff.). Since, so far, only four volumes of this edition have appeared, all quotations from the letters are from *Grabbes Werke*, ed. Spiridion Wukadinowić (Berlin: Bong, [1912]). All volume numbers from I to IV refer, therefore, to the former edition, and all numbers from V onward to the latter.

My own interest in Grabbe goes back to 1963, when I spent a summer in Detmold, the site of the *Grabbe-Archiv*. I would like here to express my appreciation to Professor Alfred Bergmann, the founder of the Archive, for his help then and in the years following. I would also like to express my thanks to the Horace H. Rackham Graduate School of the University of Michigan for the grants that made my research there, and ultimately this book, possible. I am furthermore indebted to Professor Ulrich Weisstein for his aid and assistance as General Editor.

R. C. C.

Chronology

1801   December 11, Grabbe is born in Detmold.

1805   Death of Schiller.

1807   Grabbe enters the public school in Detmold.

1812   Enrolls in the Gymnasium in Detmold.

1813   Publication of Adolf Müllner's *Schuld*, a "tragedy of fate" that strongly influenced Grabbe's first published drama and probably the two unpublished, lost plays that preceded it. Birth of Georg Büchner, Richard Wagner, Otto Ludwig, Friedrich Hebbel, and Søren Kierkegaard. Death of Christoph Martin Wieland, the last great writer of the German Enlightenment.

1815   "The Hundred Days": Napoleon's return from Elba and his ultimate defeat at Waterloo.

1816   Grabbe is confirmed in the Lutheran church at Detmold.

1817   Sends his manuscript of "Theodora" to the publisher G. J. Göschen, who returns it less than two months later.

1818   Asks his father for Shakespeare's works.

1819   Begins work on *Herzog Theodor von Gothland*, part of which is an adaptation of an earlier effort, *Der Erbprinz*.

1820   Graduates from the Gymnasium. Registers at the University of Leipzig.

1821   Death of Napoleon on Saint Helena.

1822   Clostermeier sends Grabbe a copy of his book on Arminius. Grabbe leaves the University of Leipzig and registers at the University of Berlin, where he meets Heine, Uechtritz, and others who will later become famous literary personages. He completes *Herzog Theodor von Gothland* and *Scherz, Satire, Ironie und tiefere Bedeutung*, both of which he reads to fellow students and sends to Ludwig Tieck.

1823   Completes *Nannette und Maria*. Works on *Marius und Sulla*. Reads aloud scenes from his *Don Juan und Faust* to an actor in Leipzig. In March he goes to Dresden to see Tieck and tries to become an actor. First publication: "a biographical note" for the Dresden *Merkur*, No. 42, on Ludwig Pustkuchen, a Detmold businessman. Leaves Dresden for Brunswick and later for Hanover. Finally arrives in Detmold.

1824   Takes and passes bar examination and begins a modest legal practice.

1826   Becomes assistant to the *Auditeur* Rotberg.

1827   Begins to write again after three years of inactivity: two scenes from *Don Juan und Faust*. Kettembeil's letter and the subsequent publication of the *Dramatische Dichtungen* in two volumes containing *Gothland, Scherz, Satire, Ironie und tiefere Bedeutung, Nannette und Maria, Marius und Sulla,* and *Über die Shakspearomanie.* Plans a work on Eulenspiegel and on the Hohenstaufen. Continues work on *Don Juan und Faust.*

1828   After Rotberg's death, Grabbe becomes *Auditeur.* Completes *Don Juan und Faust.*

1829   Review of the *Dramatische Dichtungen* appears in the *Foreign Quarterly Review* (England). Publication of *Don Juan und Faust,* which is performed with incidental music by Albert Lortzing. *Kaiser Friedrich Barbarossa* is published, as are excerpts from *Aschenbrödel.* Grabbe completes *Heinrich VI* and begins work on *Napoleon.* Proposes marriage to Louise Clostermeier but is rejected.

1830   Relations deteriorate with Kettembeil, who reluctantly prints *Heinrich VI* but refuses to publish *Aschenbrödel.* Grabbe suffers from gout. Revolution of 1830 in France, spreading to Belgium and Luxemburg. *Napoleon* is completed. The revolution in Poland begins. More excerpts from *Aschenbrödel* printed.

1831   *Napoleon* published. Grabbe commences *Kosciuszko.* End of Grabbe's relationship with Henriette Meyer, to whom he was engaged for a short time.

1832   Goethe's death. Death of Adolf Grabbe (born 1765).

1833   Grabbe marries Louise Christiane Clostermeier (born 1791).

1834   Publication of Ludolf Wienbarg's *Aesthetic Campaignes, Dedicated to Young Germany.* Grabbe suffers from a serious illness and increased marital difficulties. Gives up his position as *Auditeur.* Reads to his friend the beginning of his novel *Ranunder* which is lost. Leaves Detmold for Frankfurt am Main. Kettembeil refuses to publish *Hannibal,* and the friendship is dissolved. Grabbe writes to Karl Immermann, who procures quarters for him in Düsseldorf. Revision of *Aschenbrödel* is completed; revision of *Hannibal* begins.

1835   Publication of *Aschenbrödel. Hannibal* completed. Grabbe writes *Der Cid.* He sends Immermann his translation of parts of *Hamlet* and writes many reviews. Begins *Hermannsschlacht.* Henriette Husemann, née Meyer, dies. Publication of Karl Gutzkow's *Wally, die Zweiflerin,* followed by the prohibition of writings by the Young Germans Gutzkow, Wienbarg, Laube, Mundt, and Heine.

1836   Grabbe's illness increases. He borrows money from his friend Moritz Petri, in order to return to Detmold. Publication of the short sketch "Konrad" in the *Düsseldorfer Fremdenblatt. Hermannsschlacht* completed but not published until 1838. September 12, Grabbe dies.

CHAPTER 1

Christian Dietrich Grabbe:
The Man and the Legend

> Grabbe belongs to the outcasts, and petty men and
> women think he could have been different, if only
> he had wanted to be. But I say: he could not have
> been one bit different than he was, and he suffered
> enough for the fact that he was that way. The
> obligation of the living is, however, to hold the
> dead above the flood of mediocre gossip and opinion
> that reduces everything to its own level.
> —Karl Immermann[1]

DURING the nineteenth century, the interest in Grabbe's
personal life threatened to obscure any genuine interest
in his poetic works.[2] His fate bears comparison to that of the
medieval poet Tannhäuser, whose life and the superstitions
surrounding it produced the famous ballad and other accounts
of his supposed sojourn with Venus. For most of Grabbe's contemporaries, his Venus was alcohol. There were even a few
malicious people who attributed Grabbe's early death to a
disease supposedly contracted by a far more earthy "Venus."
The latter belief, however, has never been substantiated, and
his drinking now appears to have been a symptom rather than
the illness itself. Be that as it may, Grabbe was soon regarded
as the typical dissolute poet who cannot adjust to society and
dies of his own excesses. Countless novels and plays have been
written about him. Even in the twentieth century the fame—
or infamy—of his personal life continued to exert its attraction:
although they could have traced their artistic heritage, both in
technique and content, to Grabbe, the Expressionists were
primarily interested in his life as a fellow sufferer.[3] Or like
Hanns Johst, who created a fictitious portrait of him in the
drama Der Einsame (1917), they saw in Grabbe almost the
real-life predecessor of the poetrevolutionaries depicted in their

13

own dramas, as in, for example, Reinhard Sorge's *Der Bettler* (1912). Such was both the life and drama of Grabbe that usually he has found his strongest admirers among literary revolutionaries.

Yet despite the fact that Grabbe's works were of a more truly revolutionary nature, his supposed personal rebellion against the world has exercised such a strong appeal that it has probably drawn many readers to his works who might otherwise not have heard of them. It is, therefore, altogether proper and necessary to recount briefly what Grabbe actually did and to indicate what contributed to his popular image.

The purpose of this chapter is not to debunk the myths surrounding Grabbe's personality—many of them have some foundation in fact. Yet anyone who reads the accounts of his contemporaries, as well as his own statements about himself, cannot suppress the feeling that the legend about Grabbe was perhaps not in the least a product of his own intentions. Perhaps we may even view this legend as a creative work, not unlike a role he created for himself. Our interest in Grabbe's life is, therefore, not due solely to its importance as a means of interpreting his works—in the sense, for ' example, that one applies Goethe's famous words that everything he wrote was only a "fragment of a great confession." It is also due to the fact that his life was, itself, an artistic creation. As we shall see, Grabbe tried repeatedly to become an actor. Perhaps he was more or less an actor all of his life.

These speculations should not be construed to mean that we cannot know anything about the "true" Grabbe, nor that there is no important link between his personality and his works. They are intended merely to suggest an additional perspective we must apply in studying Grabbe's life. For whether he was or was not playing a role, the historical person manifested so many paradoxes, often suffered so deeply and could so frequently belie, through his conduct, the legends about him, that we realize that his character was far more complex than even Shakespeare, whom he so greatly admired, could have created.

I   *The Early Years*

Grabbe was born on December 11, 1801 in Detmold (Westphalia), at that time the capital of the Duchy of Lippe. He died on September 12, 1836 in the same city, which he often left and to which he was always forced to return. His short life span and the misery in which he spent his last months have unquestionably greatly contributed to the formation of the Grabbe legend.

From the beginning, Grabbe's life was surrounded by bizarre circumstances. His father was the warden of the local jail.[4] About this environment Grabbe said later: "What is supposed to become of a person whose first recollection is that of having taken an old murderer for a walk in the fresh air!" (cited by Immermann, p. 55). It will always remain doubtful to what extent his childhood surroundings really contributed to the character of his works and to his own personality. But Grabbe himself did little to banish his rather grotesque image from his contemporaries' thinking. Indeed, as the quotation reveals, he often seemed to encourage the formation of a Grabbe legend about his bizarre character—for at that time there was no murderer in the jail.

Grabbe owed his education largely to the wish of his parents that he should someday enter the clergy. He attended the Gymnasium in Detmold, where geography and history were his favorite subjects. He also learned Greek, Latin, French, English, and later some Italian. Even as a child, Grabbe was a voracious reader whose reading ranged from the best (Plutarch) to the worst contemporary trivial literature. It was supplemented by frequent visits to the local theater, about which he seemed, from all accounts, to have been very enthusiastic.

While still in school, Grabbe wrote his first two dramas, both of them lost. *Theodora,* the first work, was sent to G. J. Göschen, "the publisher of Germany's masterpieces and the patron of Schiller," as Grabbe described him in the accompanying letter of July 28, 1817. This description of Göschen anticipates Grabbe's subsequent identification of himself with Schiller. Later this identification will be based on a feeling of mutual suffering; here, however, it indicates the unbridled ambition that belongs to Grabbe's legendary image. Needless to say, the fledgling dramatist's work was rejected. About his second drama, *Der Erbprinz* (The Prince's Heir), we know with certainty only the title, but it is generally assumed that several passages from it were taken over for *Herzog Theodor von Gothland* (Duke Theodore of Gotland), completed five years after *Theodora.*

Of all of Grabbe's early letters, the most revealing is probably

that of February, 1818, in which he tells his father that he
has ordered a book:

The question whether the book is worth ordering is superfluous. —In
all my books you can read the praise of its author. In its own way it
is the first book of the world and is considered by many to be more
important than the Bible, for it is the book of kings and of the
people; it is the book about which some assert that a god wrote
it; it is:
                    the Tragedies of Shakespeare
which have been known for three hundred years and are by the
author of *Hamlet*. Germany owes its education to these works, for
they first excited Goethe, the greatest German; they were the ones
that prompted Schiller to travel to Stuttgart after he had attended
readings from them and inspired him to write *Die Räuber*; you can
therefore excuse me for being so impressed by them. . . .I can only
write (besides law or medicine, which I shall perhaps study) what
Shakespeare did: dramas. —With *one* tragedy one can earn fame among
emperors and royalties in the thousands. And through Shakespeare's
tragedies one can learn to write good ones, for he is, as Schiller
says, the first one whose plays have made women give premature
birth. (V, 227)

The rejection of his earlier efforts did not discourage Grabbe.
And although he had just turned sixteen, he had already decided
to devote himself exclusively to drama. Shakespeare was his
avowed model. Consequently, no small part of the literature
on Grabbe has dealt with the influence of the English dramatist—with reference to the above passage—even though Grabbe
later publicly declared his independence from, as he called
it, the "Shakespeare-mania" of the times.[5] The image of a pre-
cocious, enthusiastic, determined genius which the above letter
evokes became, in any case, an essential part of the Grabbe
legend.

Grabbe graduated from the Gymnasium in 1820. His teachers
had stated a year earlier, however, that he was "in terms of
knowledge but not in terms of his age, from which one fears
youthful outbreaks, mature enough for university studies."
Their concern was both well founded and useless for he experienced just such "youthful outbreaks" for the rest of his life.

II *The Student Years, 1820-1823*

On May 5, 1820, Grabbe entered the University of Leipzig,
where he intended to study law. He was primarily interested

in the historical aspects of his new field, partly by nature, but mainly because he hoped someday to become the archivist for the Lippe archives. Consequently Grabbe mainly attended lectures on history and philosophy. He also continued to read a great deal and attended the theater regularly.

Neither in Leipzig nor elsewhere did Grabbe ever join a fraternity. Nevertheless, he seemed to have no difficulty finding companions. Indeed, while he was at the University of Leipzig he contracted the friendship which was to prove all-important for his literary career: that with Georg Ferdinand Kettembeil, who would later inherit a publishing house and become Grabbe's first publisher. To be sure, Grabbe, according to Ziegler, frequently indulged in drinking to excess and was a frequent visitor to houses of ill-repute.

At Easter, 1822, Grabbe transferred to the University of Berlin. The most important member of the faculty was G. F. W. Hegel, who during Grabbe's first year there, was lecturing on his philosophy of history. Much has been made of this coincidence by many critics, particularly F. J. Schneider, who has tried to find affirmation of the Hegelian concept of history in Grabbe's dramas. In view of Grabbe's previous interest in history and philosophy while in Leipzig, it is altogether reasonable to assume that he might feel drawn to Hegel's lectures. But there is no evidence in Grabbe's letters that he felt any attraction to the great philosopher. Anyway, if the so-called Kant crisis of Schiller and Kleist and the "Feuerbach experience" of Gottfried Keller typify the influence of a philosopher on a poet, we may say that the philosopher usually only verbalizes the thoughts, suspicions, or doubts already present in the poet's mind. Nothing in Grabbe's letters before this time indicates that he would be receptive to Hegel's philosophy because it would satisfy any emotional or intellectual need. Nor, as we shall see, is Grabbe's presentation of history in his works "Hegelian." Another important member of the faculty at that time was Wilhelm von Humboldt, whose philosophy of language might have interested Grabbe. Unfortunately, however, there is no reference to him in the young student's letters or the later dramas. As far as Grabbe's later works are concerned, the greatest benefits he derived from his years in Berlin were not philosophical but artistic.

Grabbe's visits to the theater continued in Berlin. In the

Schauspielhaus, for example, he saw the great Ludwig Devrient
in several roles, among them that of Shylock in *The Merchant
of Venice*, and his impression of this performance might have
influenced his portrayal of the Jew Isaac in *Aschenbrödel*.
Grabbe's own production increased greatly, perhaps under the
effect of his newly acquired cultural contacts or, possibly, because of the flagging interest in his studies. In any case, *Gothland*, his first extant work, was completed on June 11, 1822.

This play gave the young man from Detmold the opportunity to demonstrate his talents to other young writers and
students in Berlin, among them, Heinrich Heine, who would
later become the subject of rumors that made him no less scan-
dalous than Grabbe. In his *Memoiren*, Heine many years later
recorded his reaction to Grabbe and his work:

I want only to note here that the aforementioned Dietrich Grabbe
was one of the greatest German poets and, of all our dramatic poets,
may be called the one who has the greatest kinship with Shakespeare.
He may have fewer strings on his lyre than others who, therefore,
perhaps surpass him, but the strings he possesses have a sound found
only in the great Englishman's works. He has the same sudden effects,
the same natural sounds with which Shakespeare frightens, moves,
and charms us. But all his good qualities are obscured by a lack
of taste, cynicism, and wildness that exceed the maddest and most
disgusting things a brain has ever produced. It is, however, not a
sickness, like fever or idiocy, for example, that produced those things,
but rather the mental intoxication of genius. Just as Plato very
appropriately called Diogenes an insane Socrates, one could call
our Grabbe—unfortunately, with twofold justification—a drunken
Shakespeare.[6]

Heine also mentions that he took the first version of *Gothland*
to Rahel von Varnhagen, who afterward demanded that he
take it back; with it in the house, she said, she could not even
sleep peacefully. And Heine himself comments: "That is the kind
of impression Grabbe's productions made in their original
form" (p. 470). In Heine's own description of Grabbe we are
struck by the combination of admiration and disgust which
the latter's drama produced in most of his Berlin acquaintances.
We also note the phrases "mental intoxication of genius" and
"a drunken Shakespeare," which helped form the legend of
Grabbe as an irrational rebel against literature and society.

And in another passage Heine himself calls the dramatist from Detmold "that foolish, peculiar fellow" (p. 470).

Gothland also furnishes an important document of Grabbe's intellectual development and the forces that played a role in it. On September 21, 1822, he sent a copy of his play to Ludwig Tieck, the famous Romantic poet, known also as the patron and editor of younger poets. Naturally Grabbe hoped for a favorable judgment. Tieck's answer, later printed in the first edition of the drama, expresses the same combination of attraction and revulsion as Grabbe's friends in Berlin showed toward both his work and his person. On the one hand, Tieck finds passages "that I would like to call great, verses from which true poetic power shines forth", and on the other, he says of it "that to a certain extent it only intends to shock, indulges in horrible, cruel and cynical matters and thereby ironicizes not only those gentle feelings but also all feeling and life in the play; yes, it even destroys the cynicism itself" (I, 3). In summarizing his judgment, Tieck writes: "And the result: your work has attracted me, interested me greatly, repulsed and frightened me and gained my great sympathy for the author" (I, 5). The fact that Grabbe had this letter reprinted indicates that he was not averse to being considered the *enfant terrible* of the literary world.

Although unsuccessful in finding a publisher for *Gothland*, Grabbe quickly followed it up with a comedy, *Scherz, Satire, Ironie und tiefere Bedeutung* (Jest, Satire, Irony, and Deeper Significance), completed in September, 1822. Here the pronounced influence of Tieck's fantastic comedies, such as *Der gestiefelte Kater*, can be felt. With this comedy began Grabbe's efforts—present, to a greater or lesser extent, in almost all of his subsequent works—to satirize his mediocre contemporaries. (Some latent satire had been present in *Gothland*, but it had been neither as bitter nor as pointed as it would later become even in the more serious works.) His definite schooling on Tieck's literary satires and his later references to Tieck give credence to the statement that Grabbe made in answer to the former's criticism: that he was "charmed to have been worth your criticism" (V, 241).

As yet, however, Grabbe had published neither work. Although his more tangible hopes for success during the Berlin years were not materializing, his letters show that he had come to a new awakening. On November 29, 1822 he wrote to his parents:

I have never had so much recognition as I have now; in a backward little town like Detmold the people cannot understand me, and I have to waste away like wilted foliage; here my acquaintances show consideration for my flaws because they realize that these same flaws stem from my positive attributes. A writer here said about me that I was a person who would not be understood until centuries later. (V, 240)

In this passage are the three motifs that characterize most of Grabbe's letters for the rest of his life: his desire for recognition, his contempt for Detmold and its provincialism, and his belief that he was destined to be understood in the future.

Grabbe's stated conviction that his weaknesses stemmed from his strength could be regarded merely as a rationalization of his inability to adjust to his environment. But this attitude certainly played a significant role in the Grabbe image; for example, in that the Expressionists, who often saw a causal relationship between excess and creativity. Grabbe seems to justify peculiar behavior if true genius—or at least a preponderance of favorable traits—has produced it. Yet in *Scherz, Satire, Ironie und tiefere Bedeutung,* written about this time, he also satirizes personal eccentricities as a means of concealing a total lack of talent. In this comedy, the Schoolmaster says to his pupil, a farm boy who is to be presented to the local nobility:

Either you must keep your trap completely shut—then they think, by Jove, that fellow must have a lot to be silent about, for he doesn't say a word;—or you must talk nonsense—then they think, by Jove, that fellow must have said something profound, for we, who otherwise understand everything, don't understand it;—or you must eat spiders and swallow flies, then they think, by Jove, that fellow is a great man . . . for not even flies and spiders revolt him. . . . Before you leave the house, you stick a dead cat in your watchpocket; afterwards when you are taking a walk with a beautiful young lady and are observing the stars in the twilight with her, you suddenly pull the dead cat out of your pocket and put it to your nose, as if you wanted to blow the latter; then the girl will grow pale as a corpse and scream, "My goodness, a dead cat." You, however, answer absentmindedly, "O my, I thought it was a constellation!" Something like that gives you a reputation for being original.

Grabbe is, of course, attacking many of his contemporaries and particularly their Romantic cult of genius and eccentricity. Seeing Grabbe, however, only as a man self-righteous toward the faults of others and blind, or at least indulgent, toward his own would be a serious error. He actually fluctuates between self-pity and self-ridicule, between messianic zeal and cynicism, between adulation of greatness and indulgence baseness. Indeed, he did not take anything seriously all the time, least of all his own person. If much in his manner, actions and speech was, in fact, only a pose, it did not stem from either a naïve or dishonest view of the world or himself. On the contrary: as exaggerated as it seemed to his contemporaries, the contempt for himself and the world which Grabbe often expresses in letters and in his work is unquestionably sincere.

III   *The Return to Detmold: His Armistice with Society,*
1823-1834

During his stay in Berlin, Grabbe had become fully convinced of his future in the theater. After abandoning his studies, he tried his luck as an actor, first in Berlin, then in Leipzig and Dresden. Despite two letters of recommendation he had managed to pry out of Tieck, however, there was no opening for him on the stage. It must be admitted, in this case, that the failure of Grabbe's efforts was largely justified, for according to all accounts he had neither the voice nor the appearance necessary for a stage career. Bitter and disappointed, Grabbe was forced by circumstances to return to Detmold, from where on August 29, 1823, he wrote to Tieck: "My misfortune consists solely in the fact that I was not born in a large city but in an area where an educated person is considered some sort of an inferior fatted ox" (V, 260).

With no other course open to him, Grabbe took his examination in law. He passed and was subsequently admitted to the bar. In contrast to the prevalent conception of him as asocial, the records indicate that he devoted himself to his new profession with diligence and skill. This is particularly notable if one considers Grabbe's flamboyant nature and the fact that the small, tranquil Duchy of Lippe could scarcely offer legal problems of the magnitude necessary to challenge such a nature. Moreover, Grabbe had not really undertaken his law studies with the intention of settling down to a modest practice but rather in the hope of eventually becoming an archivist. In this capacity he would have been able to combine his legal training with one of his overwhelming interests—history. And the history of Lippe was far from uninteresing, quite aside from the fact that the Teutoburg Forest, which lies within the duchy, was supposed to have been the site of the battle, in A. D. 9 between Arminius and the Roman armies. Indeed, the archivist, Christian Gottlieb Clostermeier (1755-1829), had in 1822, while Grabbe was still a student in Leipzig, sent him a copy of his book on the battle, *Wo Hermann den Varus schlug* (Where Arminius Defeated Varus). This book would ultimately serve as the basis for Grabbe's last completed drama. When in September, 1826, Clostermeier proposed Grabbe as his successor, it looked as if the latter would finally achieve his goal. But although Grabbe, from all evidence, was well qualified for the position, after a long delay the petition was refused. One cannot help but speculate that Grabbe, if he had become archivist, would have had a steady income and the leisure and facilities to continue writing. He might even have been spared the itinerant, desultory life that followed.

Meanwhile, on October 29, 1826, Grabbe had taken the oath as assistant to the ailing *Auditeur* Rotberg. Rotberg's death a year later made possible Grabbe's promotion to permanent legal officer with the rank of lieutenant in the minuscule army of Lippe. Despite certain temporary difficulties, not the least of which were accidents and illness, Grabbe remained an *Auditeur* until his voluntary resignation on September 14, 1834.

For many reasons, Grabbe's personal contact with military life, as routine and unglamorous as it may have been, has more than incidental importance. First of all, many of Grabbe's later plays are famous or infamous as battle-dramas—as works in which the martial spectacle of the twentieth-century movie "epics" is anticipated. Grabbe was proud of his association with the military, and in later life, as Karl Immermann records, he still cherished his uniform. But the frequent criticism leveled against the many battle scenes as a testament to Grabbe's latent desire to "play general" has no foundation in fact.

Grabbe had been notorious for drinking during his student days in Leipzig and Berlin, and this primary cause of his earlier reputation was moderated but never completely suppressed.

Nevertheless, he never disgraced his uniform.[7] Grabbe even was an advocate of strong discipline. Contrary to the legend of his capricious, unruly nature, the facts about his military career indicate that he was a good officer and lawyer until illness made it impossible for him to keep up with the work—and there was lots of it, mostly trivial, and little pay.

Many of Grabbe's difficulties during his years back in Detmold stemmed from his attempts to find happiness in marriage. These efforts eventually culminated in his disastrous union with Louise Christiane Clostermeier, the archivist's daughter. Once rejected by her, Grabbe, in 1830, turned his attentions to Henriette Meyer. After a long engagement, Henriette broke with him, left town, and in 1832 married Gottfried Theodor Husemann. Much of Grabbe's artistic inactivity at this time is accountable to his depression over the loss of Henriette. How deeply his attraction to her affected him can be seen in the fact that in 1835, when he heard of her death, he said: "She is ... now mine, immaculate, a star over her grave." After Henriette had left him, Grabbe returned to, and married, Louise Clostermeier, who was over ten years his senior and a very strong-willed person. She thought she was marrying everything Grabbe was not, and in turn she proved quite incapable of accepting and understanding what he was. We have no reason to doubt Grabbe's sincerity with regard to either woman, but once again he contributed, this time unwittingly, to the formation of a legend: an unrequited love and an unhappy marriage with a girl of middle-class morality, a marriage that must have helped to break his ever tenuous armistice with society.

Returning to Grabbe's artistic efforts during the Detmold years, we see that, due to his many obligations as a lawyer and as a legal officer, as well as for personal reasons, the period from 1823 to 1827 represented the nadir of his creativity. He only completed *Nannette und Maria,* "a tragic play in three acts," toward the end of 1826. But this short, uninspired work—artistically insignificant and certainly, as a concession to the popular stage, untypical for Grabbe—had already been conceived by 1823 at the latest. In his letter of August 1823, in which he tells Tieck about *Nannette und Maria,* Grabbe also writes that he is still working on *Marius und Sulla* and that he is thinking about a play dealing with both Faust and Don Juan (V, 259f.). Yet all these efforts hark back to his stay in Berlin, and until

1827 Grabbe seems to have written nothing new. He seems
to have missed the stimulation and recognition he had enjoyed
as a student in the company of Heine and others. Indeed,
Grabbe's inability to write under the unpropitious circumstances
in Detmold indicates that environment and public recognition
played a greater role in the pattern of his creativity than they
do in the legend depicting him as an isolated, misunderstood,
but self-assured genius. And it could also be reasonably assumed that his professional diligence as *Auditeur* stemmed, not
so much from a conventional feeling for duty and industry,
but rather from a need to find an outlet for his frustration in
the small town.

In the spring of 1827, however, a decisive turn of events
occurred: Kettembeil, Grabbe's friend from their student days
in Leipzig, wrote to him and offered to publish his works. How
decisive this first correspondence with his old friend was for
Grabbe can be seen in a letter written to Kettembeil on July
25, 1827, in which the dramatist confesses: "and strangely
enough, who knows where I would have turned, whether I
would ever again have thought about poetry if the very remarkable circumstances had not brought us together again" (V, 281f.).
Jubilantly, Grabbe sent Kettembeil his first four works, *Herzog
Theodor von Gothland; Scherz, Satire, Ironie und tiefere Bedeutung; Nannette und Maria;* and the still incomplete *Marius und
Sulla.* In his letters regarding their pending publication, he
discusses incidentally his *Don Juan und Faust,* still in progress,
and his intention to "talk in a short pamphlet a little about the
admiration of Shakespeare that has become fashionable" (V,
282). His observations on the Shakespeare adulation of his
contemporaries were, at Kettembeil's request, included under
the title *Über die Shakspearo-Manie.*

As we learn from Karl Immermann, Grabbe's first appearance
in print did not go unnoticed:

Even more extraordinary than this appendage [Tieck's letter on
Gothland, included by Grabbe as a preface to the text] is the content
of the collection itself, with which the author, all of a sudden, like
a demon, arose out of the ground. No one had announced him, no
one had recommended him. No literary coterie had worked on his
behalf. He was suddenly there. He had not asked for permission to
come, and all the world was surprised. Legends and tales, of the
kind that traditionally are given to circulate through the literary

circles of Germany, had earlier, to be sure, been reported about a certain Grabbe, who had attended the meetings of Uechtritz, Heine, and others who were poetically active in Berlin around 1821-22. The legends, however, had already been forgotten when their hero appeared. From that mythical time it is still fresh in my memory that, after his first appearance in the Berlin poetic circle, there was supposed to have been a serious argument about the question of whether this person was crazy or a genius. (pp. 17f.)

It is, however, not unlikely that the long forgotten "legends" were revived by Grabbe's reappearance in the literary arena and that Grabbe himself, if not his works, once again became a topic of conversation in literary circles.[8]

Encouraged by the publication of his four plays, Grabbe was now full of plans. For example, in a letter of August 12, 1827, he mentions a comedy *Eulenspiegel,* on which he was working. He even sent copies of his *Dramatische Dichtungen* to Tieck and Goethe, but neither responded. The publication of these works not only stimulated Grabbe to write more; it also served as a sort of catharsis from his first period of creativity. A self-composed review for the *Halle'sche Literaturzeitung* concludes with the following statements: "It must be conceded that the author of these works has considerable objectivity and imagination; tragedy and comedy as well as the most diverse characters seem to flow with equal fluency from his pen. Nevertheless, in his works one everywhere perceives only the ruins of destroyed subjectivity; the author has created ruins, in order to build anew with their help" (V, 310). Grabbe obviously realized how "confessional" his first works must appear, and he implies that such an overindulgence was an act of literary self-irony. The merits of his self-assessment must be examined later in an interpretation of the works themselves. Here it is important to note that Grabbe was leading his reading public into expecting that his next dramas would be entirely different and that he had cut himself off from the past.

But such was not yet the case. Even before he wrote the prophecy, Grabbe had been working on his next drama, *Don Juan und Faust.* Though not finished until the summer of 1828, this play also shows many of the obviously Romantic influences so evident in his first works.. Indeed, both protagonists belong to the favorite subjects of the Romantics.

Moreover, the scope of his subject alone makes it easy to

understand why Grabbe became known for his arrogance; indeed, along with Richard Wagner and many other poets, he seems to symbolize the desire of the nineteenth century to surpass all previous ages, to create giants, to be truly universal in scope. Such ambition is often interpreted as symptomatic for the "epigones," who live in the shadow of a great age and feel themselves under the influence of their predecessors. As the interpretation of his works will reveal, Grabbe did in fact sense many of the problems of his times—particularly that of adjusting to the heritage of German Idealism, in which he could no longer believe. The duration and fervor of Grabbe's struggle against Classicism and Romanticism show how serious the problem was for him. But he was not alone: Kleist, Hölderlin, Lenau, Heine, Platen, Büchner, Immermann, Grillparzer, and many others found themselves in similar situations. And almost all of these contemporaries or near-contemporaries led equally tragic lives. Grabbe was born into a politically, as well as artistically and philosophically, troubled period in German history. Many of his personal and artistic traits can also be observed in his contemporaries because they represent a general reaction to the intellectual climate of the age. It is not Grabbe's personal and artistic arrogance, eccentricity, or rupture with traditional values that separates him from most of his contemporaries, but mainly the excessive measure of these things. The problems of the times, combined with Grabbe's own insecurity regarding his background, his continued poverty and lack of recognition, his unhappy marriage, and his obvious weakness for alcohol—we would indeed be surprised if all of these things had not left their mark.

Grabbe is known today primarily as a historical dramatist. His next plays mark the beginning of his intensive preoccupation with historical figures. To be sure, *Gothland* is a period piece, but the absence of a historically fixed atmosphere and real personages deprives it of its historical character. *Marius und Sulla* represents a far more significant attempt by Grabbe to write a truly historical drama, but it remained a fragment. The fact that he did not finish *Marius und Sulla* is, in itself, an indication that he did not yet feel prepared to write historical dramas. Nevertheless, both plays, together with the historical context of *Don Juan und Faust*, also make it clear that Grabbe's subsequent concentration on the field of history was fully anticipated and should not be viewed as a total break with his first period. Indeed, in both his artistic and personal development, Grabbe seems to be consistent mainly in his inconsistency. And, while there are recognizable phases in his development, such divisions—due perhaps to the shortness of his life, perhaps to his mercurial personality—are never very clear-cut. Grabbe did not enjoy the possibilities for change that a long life like Goethe's or Grillparzer's offered; he did not leave the confines of Germany and benefit from an "Italian experience"; he did not have a period of great success, then a rebuff like Grillparzer; and, most importantly, he did not demonstrate single-minded attention to one philosophy, subject matter, style, or genre at any time in his life.

Although Grabbe never received much public recognition, it is obvious that throughout his career, as we have noted in one of his earliest letters, he was not oblivious to it. In *Nannette und Maria* Grabbe had manifested a desire, although not a particularly fervent one, to accede to popular taste. Such a desire now motivated his return to historical drama, fortunately this time with greater artistic success. In his *Geschichte der Hohenstaufen und ihrer Zeit,* which appeared from 1824 to 1826, Friedrich Raumer created a lively interest in that period of German history. A fascination with the Middle Ages had, of course, been present from the *Sturm und Drang* through Romanticism, but it was Raumer's treatment and the attention it attracted that prompted Grabbe to undertake a cycle of six to eight tragedies dealing with the Hohenstaufen. The subject was popular, and Grabbe's project was actually not as ambitious or impractical as it might seem: by comparison, Ernst Raupach wrote a cycle of sixteen dramas that were actually performed. But Grabbe never completed more than the first two plays in the projected cycle, *Kaiser Friedrich Barbarossa* and *Kaiser Heinrich der Sechste* (both in 1829). Like most of his contemporaries, the majority of whom were merely imitating Schiller, Grabbe wrote his dramas in blank verse. Of his previous works, only *Scherz* had been in prose, and *Marius und Sulla,* though predominantly written in verse, had contained several prose scenes, particularly the mass scenes, of which Grabbe, possibly pointing to their model, had written: "Even Shakespeare never wrote better mass scenes" (V, 310). Thus, both his use of verse and his selection of the Hohenstaufen as his subject

indicate a continuation of the previous period, in which he had
been influenced by Romanticism and Shakespeare. In terms of
Grabbe's own development, the Hohenstaufen dramas are his
first complete, truly historical works, but otherwise they belong,
like *Don Juan und Faust,* to a transitionary stage during which
their author still had one foot in the past and was searching
with the other for solid ground in the future.

During the genesis of the *Hohenstaufen,* Grabbe also worked
on another comedy, *Aschenbrödel* (Cinderella), which is quite
different from his first attempt in the comic genre, at least in
its final version. Especially in its increased realism *Aschenbrödel*
reveals Grabbe's new approach toward comedy.

Besides writing dramas, Grabbe continued his sporadic activity as a critic. Although he tried to offer tangible proof for his
opinions, his criticism, like his satire, stemmed mainly from his
personal reaction to the works under scrutiny. This had been the
case with his essay *Über die Shakspearo-Manie,* in which he
had vented his anger over the inability of his countrymen to
free their thinking from Shakespeare in particular and from all
previous models in general. Out of this justifiable criticism—
perhaps not in terms of the Romantics attacked personally by
Grabbe, but certainly in terms of the "epigones" flooding the
contemporary stage—had grown an almost personal battle of
Grabbe against Shakespeare. Grabbe criticized Shakespeare as
being fallible, indeed as downright slipshod in many of his
greatest plays. But the stimulus was primarily provided by
Grabbe's personal irritation with the literature and drama of
his own age.

Such was also the background of his biting review, composed
in August and September, 1830: "Something about the Correspondence between Schiller and Goethe in the years 1794 to
1805, As Well As Something about These Two Poets Themselves and about Our Times." In this review, Grabbe views the
publication of the letters as a petty act on Goethe's part to make
Schiller look petty. It is Grabbe's conclusion that Goethe was
blessed from birth with everything for which Schiller had to
work hard. Just as Grabbe's critical remarks on other poets are
colored by his personal opinions regarding their personalities,
in his judgment of Schiller he was guided primarily by a comparison between the latter's laborious path to fame and recognition and his own. His attitude toward Schiller was, however,

but another reflection of the feelings he evidenced in his dramas. In his life and in his works, Grabbe showed less empathy with the poor and downtrodden in a social sense than did, for example, Georg Büchner. But he always felt a great deal of compassion, or was moved to bitter irony, by the fate of oppressed, betrayed, or unrecognized genius, be it artistic, military, or political.

Characteristically, Grabbe's critique of Goethe is usually negative in regard to the later period, but it is often positive in dealing with the earlier works. It could, of course, scarcely be expected that a man of Grabbe's temperament would feel strongly drawn to classical works like *Iphigenie auf Tauris*. But his attack on Goethe's personality and his preference for the earlier works also seem to stamp him as a child of the times. In fact, his value judgments seem to align him with the so-called Young Germans and particularly with Ludwig Börne and Wolfgang Menzel (later in life, Grabbe even wrote a letter to the latter asking for help). But otherwise Grabbe had little in common with the Young Germans, who were motivated mainly by political considerations. On June 21, 1836, in a letter written to Petri, Grabbe recalls his stand against them and their most influential representative: "Gutzkow and Young Germany have become the subject of disdain and will not save themselves from it because they have no talent. They also wanted to snare me. I escaped, yet this novel [Gutzkow's *Wally, die Zweiflerin*] is totally insignificant, and only through this pamphlet [Gutzkow's novel] it will get the kind of notoriety in which financial speculators, professors among them, may be interested" (VI, 175).

One of the high points of Grabbe's career was reached in 1831 with the publication of his first major drama, *Napoleon oder die hundert Tage*. Although he had originally conceived the work in terms of the title figure, Napoleon soon began to lose his dominant role as Grabbe progressed with writing it. When it finally appeared, the play represented a panoramic picture of the times that took little account of the personal aspects of Napoleon's greatness. By implication, the drama extends back to the beginnings of the French Revolution and forward to Grabbe's own time. To what extent the French Revolution, even before Napoleon's emergence, occupied Grabbe's thinking is obvious from the fact that he even contemplated writing a play on Robespierre.

Napoleon is Grabbe's first serious drama written completely in prose. As Grabbe admits in his letter to Kettembeil of July 14, 1830: "For that reason, as much as it hurts me, I am writing it in—prose. But as I hope, in biblical prose, powerful as Luther's, like, for example, *Die Räuber*. I cannot force the artillery trains, the Congreve rockets, etc., into verse without making them ludicrous" (V, 345). Once again we note Grabbe's proximity to the young Schiller and Goethe (the latter's *Götz von Berlichingen* is one of the most famous dramas written in Luther's biblical style). Grabbe's *Napoleon* is, however, no historical anachronism but rather the most courageous attempt of the age to portray the revolution and its greatest "son." Obviously, we will have to compare Grabbe's drama with the other great contemporary play about the French Revolution, Büchner's *Dantons Tod*, written only four years later, and probably inspired by Grabbe's pioneering efforts. But in discussing Grabbe as an individual, we must realize that, unlike Büchner, he was not drawn to the revolution by his own interest in politics; nor did he want to make the drama a vehicle for his own attitudes. For that reason, his accomplishment seems all the more impressive.

Grabbe was, of course, living during an age of political unrest. He, too, was moved by the failure of the Revolution of 1830. In his letter to Kettembeil of September 12, 1830, he writes:

The world events that are now roaring forth like melted glaciers and which I honestly had prophesied almost in detail the case of France and Belgium, these events will be of use to us in as far as their thunderings will drown out the miserable chirp of Raupach, the coquettish warbling of Miss Sontag, [and] the reviewing of every shopkeeper's clerk whose hand itches. . . . Seriousness will count; and I have offered them seriousness and shall offer it to them again. To be sure, politics are now the main thing; but I, too, am political. (V, 349f.)

When Grabbe calls himself "political," however, he does not mean that he is so in a tangible, practical way, for he never belonged to any political party. He means only that his works deal with political issues, past and present. Grabbe also indicates no intention of joining one of the many political groups, for he considered even the current revolutions primarily from the standpoint of his own poetic works. The events in France and Belgium interested Grabbe because they gave him an advantage over Raupach and other contemporary dramatists. Although *Napoleon* did not bring him the recognition he had hoped for, it remains one of the best dramatizations of the period in any language. But the political aspects of his play lack the almost "confessional" overtones they have in *Dantons Tod*. As a matter of fact, on January 15, 1831, in a letter to Menzel, Grabbe as much as dismissed political revolutions: "All political revolutions, however, do not help at all, if each person does not revolutionize himself, i.e., does not become true to himself and others. This is the basis for all virtue, for all genius" (VI, 14). Thus Grabbe was an individualist, in principle as well as in fact, and he stood alone politically as well as artistically. It would, therefore, be a grave mistake to count him among the Young Germans or any other group, not in the least, perhaps, because their revolutions did not go far enough.

In terms of stage technique, *Napoleon* represents a complete break with most of his previous works. And Grabbe himself realized that he had not only broken with his own past, but had also defied the theater of his time: "*Napoleon* will be extraordinary—the present theater is not worth anything—let mine be the world" (V, 348). In order to re-create his gigantic subject he seemed ready to renounce, at least temporarily, any chances for popularity on the contemporary stage—another indication that he had entered a new phase in his personal and artistic development.

Grabbe's apparent contempt for the stage might have been the occasion for his beginning a novel, *Ranunder*. Unfortunately, no portions of the novel have been recovered. We know only that on October 3, 1834, he read the beginning to his friend and subsequent biographer, Karl Ziegler. Most critics concede, however, that narrative prose was scarcely Grabbe's forte, a fact substantiated by his own reluctance to complete the novel. His only other serious excursion into this form was an introduction to, and interpretation of, Edward Hartenfels' *Grupello* (published in 1840 and reprinted in Bergmann's critical edition of Grabbe's works). Grabbe's one extant prose narrative, "Konrad," is only a very short sketch that shows even less detail than the prose summaries of the unfinished parts of *Marius und Sulla*. In denying Grabbe's ability to write an extended narrative, most critics base their judgment, however, on Grabbe's personality, which they consider too unsteady, mercurial, and restive for the completion of such a work. It is ironic that Tieck once suggested that Grabbe's personality made him unsuitable as dramatist. Anyway, one could respond that Grabbe's personality would scarcely have allowed him to write a long novel of the conventional sort, mainly because he never really wanted —aside from *Nannette und Maria*—to write conventionally. Ultimately, whether or not his personality would have produced a good novel is less important than the fact that it sought to express itself dramatically, both on and off the stage. Indeed, as R. A. Nicholls quite correctly points out, even as a correspondent Grabbe more or less conversed rather than reported.

We note that Grabbe's artistic progress till now must have been accompanied by an inner turmoil. Frustration, hopes, experiments, and new frustrations had filled his thinking. Nevertheless, he had been able, despite his illness and unhappiness in love, to maintain his position as *Auditeur*. On September 14, 1834, however, he finally resigned his office. The generosity accorded to him in the form of a six-month sick-leave attests to his success. But his petition for a modest pension to allow him to write full time was rejected. On the morning of October 4, 1834, freed of his official commitments but without any real source of income, he left "that accursed Detmold" for Frankfurt am Main.

IV   Another Attempt to Escape from Detmold: Frankfurt and Düsseldorf, 1834-1836

Grabbe now hoped to make his living as a writer. His hopes were not entirely unfounded, for, carrying with him the manuscript of *Hannibal*, his second great historical drama, he was on the way to his friend Kettembeil. But his relationship with Kettembeil, whom he had once hailed as his savior, had worsened. Although he was willing to publish Grabbe's newest work, Kettembeil now made demands that led to a complete break between them.

Grabbe remained in Frankfurt. He spent several weeks in a small room, mostly in bed. During this period of desperation, his illness took a turn for the worse, and the monotony was broken only by the repeated visits of his friend Eduard Duller. Finally his fortunes had reached such a low point that he had to seek help outside. Grabbe turned to Wolfgang Menzel, who had praised his work, but without even waiting for an answer from him, he also wrote to Karl Immermann.

Immermann, who was now the director of the Düsseldorf Stadttheater, had met Grabbe briefly in Detmold and remembered him. He invited him to come to Düsseldorf, but not without some misgivings. Many years later Immermann wrote in his *Memorabilien*: "I must also confess that I felt some reluctance to let myself in for such an eccentric nature in the close association he desired. My other duties were already almost too much for me; and it would have seemed advisable not to add any new complications such as are usually caused by a homeless, unstable person. There was no close relationship between us" (p. 7). Nevertheless, Grabbe arrived on December 9, 1834, scarcely three months after leaving Detmold. Immerman recalls his impression of his new charge:

If an inhabitant of the moon fell on the earth, he would seem about as alien to the others as did my erring knight of poetry. The parts of his body did not go together. Although fine and delicate—his hands and feet were so small that they seemed to me almost underdeveloped —he moved in angular, rough and clumsy movements: His arms did not know what his hands were doing, and the torso and the feet were often at cross purposes. These contrasts reached their pinnacle in his face. He had a forehead that was high, oval, elevated, and of a splendor I have seen only in Shakespeare's picture (which is admittedly unhistorical). Under it were large, ghostly sockets and eyes of a deep, soulful blueness, and a delicately fashioned nose. Down to that point—aside from the thin, fawn-colored hair that only sparingly covered several spots—everything was quite nice. And from there on down everything was ugly, confused, unharmonious. A flaccid mouth hung peevishly under his chin, which could scarcely be distinguished from his neck. Indeed, the entire lower part of his face receded just as shyly as the upper part protruded freely and proudly.

At first Immermann represented the guiding hand the sick and run-down dramatist needed. He found a room for his unusual visitor and paid the rent for the first winter. He even made him promise to give up his morning rum—by this time no mean feat. Among the acquaintances Grabbe made through

Immermann was Carl Georg Schreiner, who had already offered to publish *Hannibal*. During this period Grabbe regained some of his vigor and creative powers. At Immermann's suggestion he rewrote *Hannibal* in prose. In this form the play appeared in 1835. In the same year, *Aschenbrödel*, which Kettembeil had refused to publish, was printed by Schreiner, also after extensive revisions. Beginning in December, 1834, Grabbe was also writing articles for the *Düsseldorf Fremdenblatt*, mainly reviews of productions at the municipal theater. In 1835 they were published by Schreiner as *Das Theater zu Düsseldorf mit Rückblicken auf die übrige deutsche Schaubühne*.

As can be seen from a list of his works prepared on July 27, 1835, probably for Schreiner, Grabbe also planned dramas on Alexander the Great and Christ, which, like *Kosciuszko*, were destined to remain fragments. Only the play on the Polish revolutionary hero can be considered more than a mere sketch.

These three fragments do, however, allow some insight into Grabbe's character: Alexander was the subject of many dramas written at this time and would naturally have appealed to Grabbe in the same way as Hannibal had. Christ seems a somewhat less likely subject for a play by Grabbe, who, although confirmed as a Lutheran and once intended for the clergy, scarcely revealed anything akin to conventional religious feelings or interests. As a matter of fact, Immermann even felt it necessary to comment on Grabbe's attitude toward religion: "In many cases of confusion and dissoluteness the belief in revealed religion proves to be a strong source of strength. Grabbe had to do without this aid. His religiosity (which is present in every person) was natural piety, absorbed in the dark forest shadows of the glorious mountains of his home." Detmold does indeed lie in beautiful, wooded hills and mountains that might have inspired a Romantic poet like Eichendorff. But such natural inspiration cannot be discerned in Grabbe's work. A love of nature on his part could be posited only on the basis of *Die Hermannsschlacht* (The Battle of Arminius), on which Grabbe had been working in Düsseldorf and which undoubtedly led Immermann to overstate the Detmold poet's attraction to nature.

Grabbe's Christ play, if completed, would unquestionably have had more in common with his *Hannibal* than with the mystical "salvation dramas" of Romanticism. In fact, we might have expected an attitude toward the Messiah not unlike that displayed by Nietzsche: an agnostic's admiration for the voluntary sacrifice of a superman for the unappreciative masses. Many of Grabbe's heroes prefigure the Nietzschean superman, e.g., Sulla, Don Juan and Hannibal. Nietzsche saw in Christ the strong leader who drove the moneylenders out of the temple, and not the Pauline figure of humility and gentleness. If Grabbe's personality and his other works offer any valid criteria for speculation, then we may assume that his Christ would have anticipated Nietzsche's image of a dynamic hero. In other words, if Grabbe had had the time to complete a drama on a truly religious subject, it would probably have been just as unconventional as his other works.

In regard to *Kosciuszko*, which had been inspired mainly by Kettembeil's desire to capitalize on contemporary interest in the Polish revolution, it must be noted that Grabbe criticized the lack of heroic proportions he obviously felt necessary for a dramatic protagonist. His patent interest in superdimensional historical figures might have represented, to a large measure, a compensation for his own appearance, which, as Immermann reports, was anything but imposing. It probably stemmed at least in equal measure from his contempt for his own very unheroic times. In any case, his obsession with personal greatness helps us to understand how Grabbe, to whom all conventional values, particularly religious ones, were alien, could want to dramatize the life of Christ and Alexander the Great. It also reveals why, despite the promise of commercial success, he was unwilling to complete the drama of Kosciuszko.

Like most of Grabbe's friendships, that with Immermann was destined to be short-lived. Grabbe's unconditional demand for clarity and truth on the part of the theater critic was the most apparent reason for their initial difficulties. Due to Grabbe's reviews, their association had already begun to disintegrate when, in July, 1835, Immermann had to leave Düsseldorf for several months. While he was gone, Grabbe, now free of any restrictions, turned increasingly to spending his time in the tavern Drachenfels. When Immermann returned in the fall, he found Grabbe completely changed and heavily in debt. By February, 1836, the rupture of their friendship was irreparable.

Looking at Grabbe's creative activity in Düsseldorf, we see that the first months allowed him to finish several previously begun works and to write his reviews. Immermann's suggestions, especially in regard to *Hannibal*, contributed greatly to shaping the final form of several works. During his stay in Düsseldorf, Grabbe also met and befriended the minor Romantic composer Norbert Burgmüller, for whom he wrote the operatic parody *Der Cid*. Burgmüller, however, died in a tragic accident before he could compose the music for the piece. The many plans attest as well to the mental vigor Grabbe had regained during the first part of his stay there.

On the debit side, however, we note that the time after Immermann lost his initial control over his "erring knight of poetry" bore little fruit. Indeed, Grabbe himself contributed to the deterioration of his health, which had never been robust. Because of his eccentric ways and cynical remarks, Grabbe made few friends among the artists in Düsseldorf. Immermann describes Grabbe's impact on others in the following passage from the *Memorabilien*: "No one could avoid the power of this very individual nature, which in no way could be incorporated into the ranks of our delicately wrinkled men of letters; he was especially effective with women, whose admiration was mixed with sympathy. I could always count on his becoming the center of interest in any company gathering around him. But it was remarkable that he inspired no love and no yearning. People occupied themselves with him only when he was present; but no one asked for him when he was not to be seen" (p. 57). If we can believe Immermann's account, it is only natural that Grabbe became almost isolated after he had lost the mediating services of his benefactor.

Whatever one can say about Immermann's relationship with Grabbe, however, it must be conceded that he was virtually the only one to understand the essential combination of seriousness and humor, of pain and nonsense, of sincerity and pose in Grabbe's quixotic nature. He praises Grabbe's unceasing jokes and "baroque" whims, yet continues: "But also in a serious way I felt myself attracted. He belonged to those people who never let anything pass their lips indifferently." And again: "In spite of all of his droll notions, in spite of his poetic outbursts, Grabbe felt profoundly miserable. His memories, like a death-breathing ghost, inspired every bloom [of wit] in him." Thus we are led to suspect that, just as his excesses were the source of his creativity, so his own seriousness and the sadness of his past generated his humor. And as we shall see later, many of his dramas do, in fact, border on tragicomedy.

After his break with Immermann, Grabbe continued his work on *Die Hermannsschlacht*, which he constantly revised and read to the few friends who were in the Drachenfels tavern or visited his sickbed. Clearly, however, his position in Düsseldorf was now no longer tenable: his illness was growing worse, his debts to Schreiner—advances on the still unfinished *Hermannsschlacht*—were so great as to be unrepayable, and there was no chance of finding a new patron. Schreiner's brother-in-law, Jakob Stang, who was also the owner of the Drachenfels, wrote a letter to Grabbe's wife, whom the latter had left behind in Detmold. He asked her to let Grabbe return to his home, but she refused. Finally Grabbe wrote to his old friend Petri, who lent him the money for the trip back to Detmold. On May 22, 1836, Grabbe left Düsseldorf. In very poor health he arrived on May 26, 1836 in the city of his birth. All he had with him was the manuscript of *Die Hermannsschlacht*.

V The Final Days in "That Accursed Detmold," 1836

Since his wife refused to see him, Grabbe stayed in a hotel. Many could see that he would never recover his health. Because his stomach could no longer stand a solid meal, alcohol had become virtually his only nourishment.

During the first few months he visited his mother—his father had died in 1832—almost every morning. But despite the pleas of his friends and his mother, he refused to enter his wife's home. He was sure that living with her again would literally mean his death, and he wanted first to complete *Die Hermannsschlacht*. At last, in July, 1836, the play was finished. Since his health had become so poor that he could no longer remain in the hotel, he went to see his wife, whose opinions had not changed. She still insisted on her right to deny her dying husband entry to the house she had inherited from her father. Finally, in the company of the police director, Grabbe gained entry to the property. For a while after he had moved into her house, he could still take an occasional walk with Petri. But soon he was no longer able to leave his bed, in which he lay totally neglected by his wife. On August 6, Louise Grabbe's patience was exhausted, and she petitioned for a divorce from her invalid husband.

Till the last, Grabbe continued to plan new works, the most significant of which was his *Till Eulenspiegel*. Through Petri he borrowed an etching of Eulenspiegel by Ramberg, about which he wrote in a letter: "The secondary characters are often well drawn, Eulenspiegel, however, has too much of Harlequin. That should not be the case, for he is no mere joker but rather represents the German world irony that has arisen from the most profound seriousness" (VI, 178). We recall Immermann's description of Grabbe and cannot help speculating that, had he been able to write this drama, it would have belonged to his greatest. Of all the poets of the time, none seemed, artistically as well as personally, more suitable to dramatize the story of Eulenspiegel, the legendary figure who, like Grabbe, had ridiculed, duped, and flaunted the philistine elements of society. If Grabbe, as a person, had literary predecessors, one was undoubtedly the earthy, ironical, and sly Eulenspiegel, and the other the most famous "erring knight of poetry," Don Quixote.

The local pastor visited Grabbe, who, however, refused the consolation of the church. On September 10 and 11, 1836, his mother tried to visit her dying son, but both times she was driven from the door by the screams and vituperations of his wife. Finally, on September 12, 1836, she gained entry, and her son died in her arms.

When he was buried four days later, only fifteen to twenty young men were in the procession. None of the prominent members of the society in the capital of the duchy were present.

VI *Epilogue*

It is obvious even from the brief account given that there is material in abundance for a Grabbe legend, which is that of an iconoclastic, misunderstood, ecstatic, and drunken poet who never ceased to wage his quixotic fight against his environment. Many of his contemporaries saw only such a figure in him. But we shall never know to what extent this impression was the calculated result of a pose that grew out of Grabbe's insecurity, fear, and inability to throw off his small-town manners. Nor is it altogether unlikely that Grabbe's eccentric behavior stemmed from a genuine belief in his own genius. Furthermore,

most of our records and accounts were set down by poets like
Heine and Immermann, or professional writers like Duller, all
of whom were interested in telling a fascinating story. And in
reading many eyewitness accounts by less skilled observers, we
note that they had been prepared by rumor and anecdote to see
an eccentric character even before they had met Grabbe. Admittedly, he seldom disappointed them.

Be that as it may, the facts of Grabbe's life show that another
misconception could easily arise—and has in fact arisen—namely,
that Grabbe, who never left Germany, was a powerful but
unsophisticated talent. Yet Grabbe was recognized by no lesser
men than Heine and Immermann. While they criticized his
personality, his intellect and his knowledge of literature were
not questioned. Not only his contact with the literary greats
of his time but also his constant visits to the theater must have
contributed to his development, for as his letters and reviews of
the Düsseldorf performances show, he had a chance to familiar-
ize himself with all of the important dramatists, past and contemporary. In theatrical matters, Grabbe was probably far more
experienced and knowledgeable than his great contemporary
Georg Büchner, whose political activities and academic interests did not leave him much time in his short life for first-
hand acquaintance with the theater. One might well say that
Grabbe's ambition was too exalted for the contemporary stage,
but one can scarcely assert that his knowledge of it was too slight.

Grabbe sensed his isolation from the intellectually insignificant contemporaries ruling the literary scene. Not only did he
refuse to abandon his ideas for safer, more conventional ones.
He tried personally to repulse rather than attract those around
him—at the cost of possible friendships with the few acquaintances of his own stature. His was a belief in his own future. His
words to Gustorff sound like an epigraph he consciously or
unconsciously stamped on his works: "I stand and keep myself in
the background. Cometh time, cometh Grabbe" (V, 252).

CHAPTER 2

The Early Works

I Herzog Theodor von Gothland. *A Tragedy in 5 Acts*

ACT I, scene 1: In an opening scene somewhat reminiscent of that of *Hamlet*, we see two Swedish watchmen guarding the coast. The settings suggest an Ossianic landscape. In the storm the Finns land invasion troops. The play is set during the early period of Christianity in Sweden, and the Finnish army, led by the African Negro Berdoa as its general and high priest, represents a primitive, heathen force in battle with Christian civilization. It is not beyond the realm of possibility that the battle between two cultures and religions was inspired by the *Nibelungenlied*. A more likely source, however, would be the preoccupation of many Romantic writers with the early stages of civilization in their so-called cultural-mythical dramas. But Grabbe goes beyond his predecessors when he adds the grotesque relationship between Berdoa and the Finns: Berdoa claims racial as well as religious kinship with the Finns in his assertion: "That [a European] the Finn is not; his race is related to mine. The Finn knows that in gray, primitive times his fathers left Asia's steppes; for years they wandered;—finally they built their huts on the eternally thundering shores of the Baltic Sea" (I, 16).

Yet Berdoa's attack on the Swedes, whom he hates as Europeans, is motivated primarily by his hatred of Gothland, Sweden's most illustrious warrior. As soon as Berdoa's personal hatred is revealed, the cultural-religious aspects of the Swedish-Finnish struggle are almost forgotten.

I,2: Berdoa and Irnak sneak into Gothland's castle, where they encounter Rolf, a servant who has brought Gothland the news of Manfred's death by a stroke. By means of trickery, murder, and coercion, Berdoa sets the stage for convincing Gothland that Manfred, his younger brother, was in fact murdered by his older brother, Friedrich, the chancellor. Among

40

other things, Berdoa has Manfred's body decapitated and the
witness to his burial murdered. Not only does the youthful
playwright seem to relish such bloody excursions into realms
of terror and shock, but he also shows how little he cares about
the more gentle art of treachery and deception as practiced
by such Shakespearean characters as Iago.

I,3: When Gothland arrives at the tomb, he believes that
Manfred was indeed the victim of murder, because Rolf, intimi-
dated by Berdoa, substantiates his suspicions by recounting—
with no dearth of gory inventions—the murder he supposedly
witnessed.

II,1: Gothland brings his grievance against Friedrich to the
King of Sweden and the nobles. Although the nobles accept
the forged evidence and find Friedrich guilty, the King sets
aside their verdict.[1]

II,2: Feeling deprived of his rights, Gothland goads the
chancellor into a duel and kills him. With his son Gustav, the
Duke flees from the wrath of the King, who banishes him, and
from his father, who swears to avenge the fratricide.

III,1: A storm on the coast of the Baltic. The many storm
scenes in this play could possibly be accounted for by Shakespeare's influence, particularly *Hamlet, Lear,* and *Macbeth.*
Gothland encounters Rolf, whom he had locked in the tomb
with Manfred's mutilated body at the end of Act I. Rolf relates
the story of his liberation by a monk—but only after telling of
his hunger, which caused him to eat the flesh from his fingers,
and of snakes that crawled into his prison. There are many
echoes of the *Sturm und Drang* in this work, and here we think
immediately of Gerstenberg's *Ugolino.* When Rolf reveals to
Gothland that his testimony was false, the latter realizes that he
has unjustly killed his brother. But he refuses to accept Rolf's
advice to do penance. This is, without question, a turning point
in the plot of this play, which Benno von Wiese has called
"the first tragedy of nihilism."

The powers of his life, Gothland says, have condescended to
lead him onto the path of evil, and he will now continue on it.
As his first consciously evil act, he then throws Rolf, the witness
of his crime, into the sea. In a long monologue, Gothland denies
God and posits insanity and malice as the guiding forces of
the universe. Berdoa appears and ridicules Gothland's pretensions of denying God. The latter is about to take revenge

on the Negro, whom he holds responsible for his crime, when the Swedish army arrives, led by the King and old Gothland.

The Finns flee, but one of their leaders, Rossan, who hates Berdoa, calls upon Gothland to become their ruler. With the help of Arboga, a Swedish nobleman once punished by the King, Gothland defeats the Swedes.

III,2: Gothland assumes the title of King for himself. The act ends with Berdoa's plot to avenge himself on Gothland by having Gustav seduced.

IV,1: The Swedish-Finnish army is encamped on the Norwegian border. Gothland expresses his despair and doubt about the meaning in existence. His disillusionment is further strengthened by Berdoa. But Gothland finally suppresses his conscience by saying that Manfred was a sentimental fool and the chancellor a "man-like dullard," who was worth even less. Cäcilia, Theodor's wife, and her father appear; but, rejecting her pleas to reform, Gothland sends them both out into the storm to die. Gustav has been seduced by Berdoa's female accomplice and now even uses the Negro's curses: he repudiates his father and seeks only carnal pleasure.

IV,2: Gothland discovers Gustav and Berdoa during a wild orgy in the latter's tent. He has his son whipped and the Negro chained.

IV,3-4: We see the death of Cäcilia in the wilds and the rescue of her father. Interspersed throughout are Gothland's wanderings and self-recriminations in the storm, during which his hair turns white.

V,I: Gothland returns to his camp, where he orders Rossan to kill Berdoa and Arboga to massacre the sleeping Finns. V,2-3: But Gustav betrays his father by alarming the Finns, who free Berdoa and thwart the plot.

V,4: Gothland is imprisoned with Tocke, who has murdered his sister and whom Gothland regards as a parodist of his own crime. Over and over again, political rather than family relationships are used by Grabbe to illustrate more universal meaning. By the strength of his desperation Gothland frees himself from the chains. V,5: Thinking only of revenge, Gothland sets out in pursuit of Berdoa, who kills Gustav during the wild chase through the camp. After Gothland has caught and killed the Negro, he feels completely apathetic. V,6: After learning that Gothland has betrayed him to the Finns, Arboga kills Gothland, who makes no attempt to defend himself. King Olaf arrives with the victorious Swedish army and finds Gothland's body, over which his father breaks down.

Finding faults in this play does not demand great critical acumen on the part of the "reader"—we can assume that a "viewer" of an uncut performance of this work will probably never exist. The drama is much too long, possibly because Grabbe was reluctant to discard entirely his two earlier, rejected plays. It also seems too long because there is too much repetition that does not move the plot, which, in terms of Gothland's development, reaches its climax in the third act.

Too many problems are created or implied for any one drama to satisfy within the limits imposed by an audience's patience. Moreover, Grabbe does not do much beyond suggesting these problems. For instance, the socio-cultural aspect is evoked, then dropped. The North-South conflict, which will, in later dramas, play a significant role, is not yet fully developed. Gothland's relationship to his family—be it the brother he loved, the brother he kills, his wife or his father and the family tradition—is treated in a cursory manner.

The language, as full of obscenities as it is by the standards of the nineteenth century, is often bombastic, and its pathos frequently becomes self-parodying in its exaggeration. In terms of the number of scenes and characters the play exceeds both the audience's comprehension and the demands of the stage. Motivations of the characters are too often missing entirely or merely suggested. One might almost say that each character is playing the part of a literary predecessor whose motivation is readily accepted. For example, Berdoa's actions do not evoke our interest in what he feels and why he feels it, but rather our curiosity as to which character in some other drama we must look for in order to understand him. Invariably the more learned reader will search his memory for parallels to a Shakespearean villain—Iago, Richard III, or Aaron in *Titus Andronicus*. And the relationship of Arboga to Gothland recalls Butler's role in Schiller's *Wallenstein*.

We feel that Grabbe, while indirectly attacking the traditional theater of his time, remains heavily indebted to it. Over and over again Gothland rejects fate and ascribes everything to "chance." Yet much of this play obviously stems from the "fate tragedies" of Grabbe's time. Particularly Müllner's *Yngard* lurks in the background but countless other plays as well—so many in fact that Otto Nieten devotes an entire section to the fate tragedy before his discussion of *Gothland*.

The deficiencies of Grabbe's first published play are so patent that naming them seems like beating a dead horse to death. But wherever we touch upon Grabbe's life and works, we find excesses on both the positive and negative sides, and here as well. *Gothland* is unquestionably a work of genius. F. J. Schneider has called it one of the great first works and ranks it with Schiller's *Die Räuber*, Büchner's *Dantons Tod*, and Hebbel's *Judith*. Such a comparison might be overdrawn, but several aspects of Grabbe's play certainly merit praise. Above all, we are favorably struck by many of the monologues, by occasional flashes of ingenuity, and by the sheer scope of the action.

Moreover, although his coordination and execution is far from mature, Grabbe introduces into this play almost all of the themes and motifs that characterize his later dramas. This fact alone makes *Gothland* an important work. Perhaps we are disturbed by the pathetic frenzy with which certain ideas are stated, but this very overstatement offers an advantage. It allows us to perceive Grabbe's attitudes more clearly than in the later plays, for which these attitudes frequently form only a background. It has been correctly stated that no single play can represent Grabbe, but certainly *Gothland* and its comic complement, *Scherz, Satire, Ironie und tiefere Bedeutung*, come as close as any to fulfilling this role.

One of the main problems Grabbe was faced with was the character of Gothland. In establishing the Duke's tragedy, he proceeds from two propositions that are substantiated by the play: (1) that great love leads to great hate, and (2) that hope alone provides the basis for any meaningful assertion of both the individual and of humanity in general.

Unlike his Austrian contemporary, Franz Grillparzer, Grabbe never showed any pronounced desire to provide an extensive psychological foundation for the actions of his characters. But to say that he neglected the problem of motivation even in this play, his first and most disorganized, would be misleading. By and large he makes Berdoa, the seducer, the comment on Gothland's psychology. For example, in Act V the Negro gloats over his completely degraded victim by telling him that he wanted to deceive himself (I, 183-85). Berdoa, however, only hints at a motif which a playwright more concerned with human psychology would have strongly emphasized: Gothland's latent envy or hate toward his brother Friedrich, whom he only too willingly accuses of Manfred's murder. More concentrated attention on such fraternal rivalry would have undoubtedly made more acceptable the fact that Gothland believes his worst enemy, Berdoa, rather than his brother. But Grabbe contents himself with the Negro's remark that Gothland loved Friedrich less than Manfred, and we must assume that if there had been an unknown flaw in the Duke's character, Berdoa would have been the one to discover and reveal it. Grabbe did not pursue the line sketched in above—the line most suitable for a credible motivation—because he was interested not in a cause-and-effect relationship but in chaotic upheaval and, to use Nietzsche's phrase, a "revaluation of all values."

Gothland's fall is not that of a conventional tragic figure with one previously unknown flaw, but rather that of the complete idealist who is seemingly flawless. Correspondingly, Berdoa plans his destruction on the premise not of a weakness but of a strength: when he hears that all of Scandinavia admires the great love of the three Gothland brothers for one another, he triumphantly asserts: "Great love, great hate" (I, 21). In other words, only he can passionately hate who once passionately loved.[2]

Berdoa's general assumption regarding the fate of the "good" man, on which his plan of intrigue was based, is substantiated. In addition to the Negro's tangible success, we have Gothland's own insight: he has become three times as evil as Berdoa because he was once good (I, 96). His own moral disillusionment acquires dogmatic proportions for Gothland when he later says: "No one has yet come into life with ideals for the well-being of humanity who did not leave it as a villain and confirmed misanthrope" (I, 146). We now realize why Grabbe spends so much time on the military and political controversies between the Swedes and Finns. Gothland's betrayal of his land is the effect of his love for it, and his reaction against the King of Sweden is conditioned by the love he once felt for him. His treachery and bloodthirstiness are so great because he was once the noblest of warriors.

Although Grabbe deals extensively with the pseudohistorical

aspects of the action, the play does not impress us as being historical. Most critics maintain that the play degenerates into a family tragedy not unlike the mediocre fate tragedies of the times. This contention bears a fair amount of credence. But the main reason for the play's lack of conviction as a historical drama lies in the fact that the sociopolitical action is subordinated to Gothland's personal disillusionment and to the effect of this disillusionment on him as a metaphysical being, not as a nobleman, brother, or soldier.

Gothland derives its tension from violent confrontations: Finns against Swedes, heathens against Christians, African against European, brother against brother, son against father, subject against king, individual against homeland, and so forth. Yet almost all these conflicts are either left unrealized in their potential or lack a clear profile of issues and decisions. They are only symptomatic of the primary conflict lying within the protagonist himself, a conflict that is, in turn, projected on all of the other events. This conflict is described by Gothland after his murder of Rolf:

Man projects the "good" into world history when he reads it because he is too cowardly boldly to admit its terrible truth to himself. No, no—there is no God; for His sake I want to believe that there isn't. . . . Man has eagles in his head, and his feet are stuck in the mud! Who was so mad as to create him? Who threw him together out of donkey ears and lion teeth? What is madder than life? What is madder than the world? It was almighty insanity that created it. . . . Fate is cruel and horrible, but it is not planned, malicious, [or] cunning! It is almighty malice that directs the course of the world and that destroys it. (I, 80-82)

Ultimately, the love-hate relationship is applied to God. Loving God is possible only as long as a benign plan can be recognized in the course of events. But such a plan lies beyond man's ken. As R. A. Nicholls (p. 58) points out, Grabbe anticipates Nietzsche's famous statement that "God's only excuse is that he does not exist." If there were a God, Gothland would resent and hate Him because he once loved Him and expected so much of Him. Such a position characterizes the so-called *Weltschmerz* of the nineteenth century. The *Weltschmerzler* had grown up in the Romantic tradition that one could intuit God; but later they could no longer accept the objective existence of their intuition.

Even during the flowering of German Romanticism one had, to be sure, heard questioning voices, the most penetrating of which had belonged to Heinrich von Kleist. It is interesting to note that Grabbe's first drama is based on a series of deceptions not unlike those encountered in Kleist's works: the more convinced the protagonist is that he has recognized the plan behind the events, the more devastating is his subsequent recognition that he has been deceived or that he has deceived himself. To the end, however, Kleist retained a faith in God that Grabbe rejected already in his first play. The disillusionment of Gothland, the idealist, symbolizes the fall of all idealism that characterizes *Weltschmerz* as a historical phenomenon.

As Gothland states, ideas are only "eagles" in man's head. Because the *Weltschmerzler* have not gained their sought-after knowledge of God but only an awareness of their own disappointment, their mind seems to them not a blessing but a curse. Gothland says: "O, how happy is an animal! It doesn't cry, it doesn't regret, and once it is dead, it doesn't live anymore" (I, 131). Consciousness and the awareness that there *should be* a God becomes their curse as men. Like Büchner's Danton, they seek forgetfulness and death as a release from their consciousness as well as from their conscience.

The model for most *Weltschmerzler* was Lord Byron, and their favorite images were those of the prison of the mind and body and of the grave, of loneliness, and of suffering. These were the poets who sought God but could not find Him, and who found themselves imprisoned in a world void of the divine. If they could never know with certainty about God, they could never know eternal, transcendental truth. Because all hope of ultimate knowledge is locked up within man himself, each man, in their view, was his own prison and was condemned to eternal loneliness. The only thing man could know for sure was his own pain or pleasure.

In the best tradition of *Weltschmerz* Gothland asserts: "Listen, a hundred thousand men are watching and keeping me company, and yet I remain lonely and alone; Oh, every mortal, and even if he sat on the throne of the most populous nation, wanders lonely among millions; no one else can understand his pleasure, his pain. And he must perish in loneliness" (I, 133). Similar statements were made by Byron, Lenau, Heine, Platen, and Büchner. In the poetry of *Weltschmerz* two figures appear over and over again: Cain and Ahasverus, the Wandering Jew, both of whom are condemned to wander forever. The moral aspects of their fate have become ontological, however, for the "Mark of Cain" has, in the early nineteenth century, come to designate not only the punishment of a crime but also the curse of consciousness itself. Actually, Gothland does not suffer so much from guilt as from disillusionment. When he sees a tired farmer returning to his hut, a man enjoying all the peace and tranquillity of the simple life, he says: "I do not understand why he deserves this beautiful lot instead of me; if he had been tempted as I have been, he, too, would have fallen" (I, 121). It is not only Gothland's political involvement and his high station but also his awareness as an individual that is responsible for his fate. We must assume that the farmer accepts life and God, but since the simple man never seeks the full measure of either, he can never be disappointed. In other words, since he does not "love" either one passionately, he can never "hate" them as passionately as does Gothland. But if the farmer had been tempted to seek God actively, he too would have suffered disillusionment.

Because they consider man deprived of hope, the *Weltschmerzler* see hope as the unobtainable goal as well as a means of man's never-to-be-achieved salvation. In talking about the farmer, Gothland says: "He has sown the last grain and *hopes* to God that it will flourish in the coming spring" (I, 121; italics mine). But this world of hope and spring is closed to Gothland, just as it is to Lenau, who usually finds himself in a somber, pale autumn landscape, and for whom bright, springlike colors appear only occasionally on the distant horizon.

Gothland's wife, Cäcilia, embodies the saving principle of hope. In the wild mountain range, symbolic of the state of affairs in Scandinavia at the time, she asserts: "Pity him who can no longer hope! Hope is ultimately the only blessing of life. For of all the great and sublime things, of God, immortality, and virtue, man does not know that they exist—he has never seen them, he has never experienced them—he can only *hope* that they are there; for that reason let us hope in life's darkness, let us hope in the deserts!" (I, 157). Hope means a belief in eternity, but Gothland—and herein lies his tragedy, the first tragedy of nihilism—has lost all hope because he can no longer believe in eternity. Cäcilia appears to her husband as, in her words, "a delegate of higher powers, of the noble, good and just." But he rejects her because he can no longer turn back. In other words, he has lost hope in penitence, divine justice and forgiveness. What he does here and now is final.

When he attacks the concept of "eternity," Gothland undermines the cornerstone of positive Romanticism. One only has to read a few poems of such Romanticists as Eichendorff to see how central "eternity" (*Ewigkeit*) is to the Romantic longing for infinity and God. For example, Eichendorff's poem on the hermit ("Der Einsiedler") closes: "O, consolation of the world, you quiet night. The day has made me so tired, the wide ocean is already darkening. Let me rest from desire and need until the eternal dawn glistens its way through the tranquil wood." The eternal dawn, the eternal rebirth, the eternal hope—they all stem from the Romantic belief in an infinite world in which God is always present.

In this context, Gothland's lines in Act III, scene 1, fix the literary-historical position of the play: "So that is man: the present dominates him, and mere change attracts him! The lesser torture, which now torments him, he gladly exchanges with an even greater one in order to get rid of it; whoever has a toothache wishes that it were a headache, and if it were a headache, he would wish for a toothache. To the man oppressed by a despot anarchy seems welcome, and the man being hanged wishes to be put on the rack!" (I, 90). In one form or the other, this belongs to the credo of *Weltschmerz*. The post-Romanticists like Grabbe, Heine, Lenau, Platen, and Büchner see man as a helpless victim of his own pain and, therefore, as a captive of the moment. Even those contemporaries who have lost faith in Romantic idealism but do not feel man to be merely a slave of his disillusionment reject eternity as a meaningful concept. For example, in Franz Grillparzer's *Ein Bruderzwist in Habsburg*, the Emperor Rudolf says: "But man lives only for the moment; what happens today worries him, and there is no tomorrow."

Gothland shares with such characters as Büchner's Danton the feeling that time is almighty: "I believe in the omnipotence and omnipresence of time! Time creates, completes and destroys the world and everything in it; yet I do not believe in a god who is greater than time; such a god cannot, may not, should not exist and does not exist!" (I, 129). For this reason, there can be no "good" revealed in history (see I, 80-82, cited above).

There is no "idea" inherent in history, and each event is lived only for its own excitement. The real world is all we have. Although *Gothland* is not a truly historical drama and its characters are far from credible as historical persons, Grabbe's emphasis on time as the only meaningful criterion forms the basis for his increasing realism. Man as a blind captive of the present time, of his present emotions and of the thrill of the moment for its own sake—this is man as he will later appear as the subject of Grabbe's truly historical dramas.

Not infrequently, however, the critics point to *Gothland* as almost an anachronism, for they see it as a resurgence of the *Sturm und Drang.* We have ourselves noted some of these echoes. In his basic attitude, however, Grabbe is far removed from the 1770's, for, as the above discussion has revealed, much of *Gothland* represents a conscious rejection of Romantic values and must be understood in a literary-historical context primarily as a document of post-Romanticism and *Weltschmerz.* *Gothland* would not have come into being if there had not been a Romantic movement.

Nevertheless, there is a recurrence of one motif from the *Sturm und Drang* that links this play, as well as certain works by other *Weltschmerzler*, with the times of Schiller's and Goethe's youth: that of Faust. All of the Faust drams of the Storm and Stress were symptomatic of the times—even the greatest of them, Goethe's. In Grabbe's time, Faust once again became the symbol of historically determined attitudes. Taken as such, the post-Romantic Faust can have little in common with that of the *Sturm und Drang.*

Many of the early nineteenth-century Faust figures are actually anti-Fausts. For example, one of the most frequently cited examples of the so-called *Biedermeier* and its fear of ambition is Grillparzer's play *Der Traum, ein Leben,* which is, in turn, dubbed an "Anti-Faust." Because the *Biedermeier* poets' glorified domesticity, resignation, and the suppression of strong feelings, they naturally felt little kinship with the promethean character of earlier Faust dramas. With what tranquil resignation, for example, Chamisso's Peter Schlemihl accepts his fate! Grabbe and the other poets of *Weltschmerz* were at opposite poles to *Biedermeier* values, and no better evidence of their opposition can be found than their obsession with Faust as a spokesman for their views. Grabbe, Heine and Lenau actually wrote, or at least began to write, their own *Faust,* and all of Büchner's works reveal traces of the Faust motif. Although having little in common with the *Biedermeier* Faust, the *Weltschmerz* Faust nevertheless bears only superficial resemblance to the figure of the *Sturm und Drang.* Biedermeier produced an anti-Faust of resignation and humility. Grabbe, using the Faust motif in *Gothland* portrays, by implication, a Faust *inversus,* a Faust revealing not man's greatness but his insignificance, not his humility in the face of this insignificance but his defiance.

Gothland has his Mephistopheles in Berdoa. But unlike Goethe's Faust, the Swedish Duke succumbs to the Mephistophelean ethic. How much Grabbe's thinking revolved around the Goethean drama is particularly patent in Act III, scene 1. Gothland says, "God is malicious, and desperation (*Verzweiflung*) is the true worship of God" (I, 82f.). Under the prodding of Berdoa he then asserts *three* times, "Creation was created because it should deteriorate" ("Weil es/ Verderben soll, ist das Erschaffene/ Erschaffen!") (I, 83). This reminds us of what Goethe's Mephistopheles says to Faust: "I am the spirit that always negates! And rightfully so; for everything that arises is fit to deteriorate" (11. 1138-40). Goethe's Faust rejects this credo, but Grabbe's Gothland accepts it.

Not only for this reason, however, can we speak of Gothland as a Faust *inversus.* From the beginning of Goethe's drama, we know that Faust will be saved, and even Mephistopheles must confess that he "always wants the bad, but always creates the good." It is a benign universe in which Faust finds himself. Gothland, on the other hand, is a victim of caprice, who knows no ideals. Faust's death will occur only when he has attained some goal that makes the future unimportant (we must remember that only *Faust I* had appeared by the time *Gothland* was written). For Gothland, the *Weltschmerzler,* there is no future, only the present. Faust will voluntarily leave life when he has achieved a positive value. Gothland dies of ennui, like Büchner's Danton, because the only meaning he can find in life is the stimulus of the moment. When he has killed Berdoa, life is no longer important. After his "fall," Gothland, who had once lived for love, is nourished by hate, disillusionment, and the pain of self-torture.

Grabbe's protagonist is able to recognize only the bad, not

the good. Consequently, his existence depends on the elimination of pain, and not on the realization of values. Before he dies, Faust will have answered a question about the universe, or at least about man's role in it. Gothland, on the other hand, receives no answer. In fact, his lot resembles that described in Heine's poem "Laß die heil'gen Parabolen," which concludes: "Thus we ask continually until our mouths are finally stuffed with a handful of earth—but is that an answer?"

Grabbe's devil, Berdoa, also belongs to the times. He is, quite simply, a savage and a brute. Nicholls is certainly right when he sees in Berdoa a renunciation of the "noble savage," who had been glorified by Rousseau and later by the Romantics. In this context, Max Spalter likens Gothland to Brecht's Baal, one of the most striking attacks on man's inherent nobility. For Grabbe, the primitive is not good and gentle, divine and innocent. Such a view of pristine innocence, advanced by Rousseau and furthered by Herder, by the Romantics and ultimately sugar-coated by the Biedermeier love of dogs and children, has no place in Grabbe's works. More and more we shall see how in Grabbe's works the primitive corresponds to the satanic, chaotic, and brutal, be it in an individual like Berdoa, or in the masses of Rome, Paris or Carthage. Just as there is no future, there is no escape into an innocent, gentle, idyllic past. Grabbe's pre-occupation with history has, therefore, nothing to do with the escapism of Biedermeier poets, who glorified "the good old days," just as it has nothing to do with the Romantic search for mythical, divine insights in man's origins.

In fact, the brutality of the play—evident in the recurring animal images of reptiles, tigers and lions as well as in the obscenity, bloodletting, and cruelty—seems to be a conscious effort to shock not only the late dreamers among the Romantics but also the complacent scribes of saccharine Biedermeier values. Moreover, the emphasis on visible brutality and on verbal shock-effects stems in no small measure from Grabbe's refusal to accept "das schöne Wort" of Goethe's and Schiller's classical dramas.

The conclusion of Gothland builds a bridge to Grabbe's next play. Apparently for no reason, Old Gothland, who is crying over his dead son, tells the Swedish King and the nobles surrounding him that they should not laugh. This groundless accusation could, of course, be merely another reminiscence of

King Lear, an obvious model for many of the details. On the other hand, the reference to laughter substantiates our feeling of the futility and absurdity of Gothland's downfall. Grabbe calls his next work a counterpart to *Gothland,* and fittingly enough, it is a comedy.

II Scherz, Satire, Ironie und tiefere Bedeutung

Act I, scene 1: The Schoolmaster has accepted one of the peasant boys as a pupil, for which service he is paid in drink. In a broad satire on the literary tastes of the time and on the pretensions of the popular expectations of a "genius," he prepares the boy for an interview with his prospective patrons, the Baron and his daughter Liddy. I,2: The Devil is sitting on a hill where, despite the summer heat, he is freezing. A passing scientist discovers him and takes him back to his colleagues in the Baron's castle.

I,3: Because the Devil does not fit into any of their systems, the scientists cannot decide what sort of creature he is, but they finally agree that such an ugly creature could only be a lady writer—a frequent target of Grabbe's satire throughout the comedy. The Devil thaws out, awakes, and tells the scientists, the Baron, Liddy, Wernthal (her fiancé), and Rattengift (a poet) that he is a clergyman. This group is joined by the Schoolmaster and his rather stupid "genius," who fools no one. Satire on prominent literary figures of the day fills much of the scene. The Devil is given a room in the castle, to which he retires. I,4: He discovers that one of the horseshoes on his feet is loose and calls the village blacksmith to have his hoof reshod. In this scene, most of the low comic possibilities of the situation are exploited.

II,1: Grabbe parodies the Devil's bargains in fable and folklore: Mordax, who wants to win Liddy, is promised help by the Devil, but only on several conditions, including the murder of twelve journeymen tailors and the breaking of the ribs of the thirteenth. The second "pact" of this scene is concluded between the Devil and Wernthal, who, after quibbling about the value of such attributes as virginity, sells Liddy to the Devil for a ridiculous sum. In order to give Liddy to Mordax, the Devil plots to have her kidnapped at a hut in the forest.

II,2: Ostensibly, this scene deals with the Devil's efforts to trick Rattengift into leading Liddy to the hut, but it also concerns the nature of Hell, Heaven, and the world, which the Devil explains to the poet. Here Grabbe again gives vent to his satire. The Devil describes Hell:

We laugh at a murderer until he has to laugh along with us because he went to the trouble of killing a human being. The severest punishment of the damned consists, however, in having to read the *Abendzeitung* and *Der Freimütige* [belletristic periodicals of the day] without being able to spit at them. . . . Not only the bad but also the pitiful comes to Hell: thus the good Cicero sits there as well as the bad Catiline. Since, today, modern German literature is the most pitiful of pitiful things, we prefer to occupy ourselves with it.

Famous characters and authors abound in Hell; for example, the Marquis Posa from Schiller's *Don Carlos* is now a panderer and owns a beer garden called the Queen Elizabeth (an allusion, of course, to *Maria Stuart*, also by Schiller). The bulk of the satire, however, is directed at truly mediocre figures of fact and fiction, most of whom are scarcely known today.

II,3: Mollfels, an incredibly ugly individual, who has always adored Liddy from afar, returns to the village. As we hear in the next scene, he is so ugly that seven old women jumped into the castle pond when they saw his face. II,4: Mollfels expounds on his ugliness and declares his love for Liddy, who is not entirely unresponsive.

III,1: Opening with a conversation between the blacksmith and the Schoolmaster, in which the latter learns the true identity of the "clergyman" and orders a cage from the smith, the scene switches to its main action: because Mollfels, after hearing that Liddy is engaged, wants to commit suicide, the Schoolmaster and Rattengift indulge in a drinking bout with him in order to console him. This is one of the comic highlights of the play.

III,2: This scene is strictly pantomime: Mordax goes for a walk, encounters thirteen journeymen tailors, puts on a napkin, and kills them.

III,3-4: These scenes are brief, episodic treatments of the three drinkers' "mornings after" and of Rattengift's attempt to persuade Liddy to accompany him to the "poetic" hut in the forest.

III,5: The Devil is captured in a cage that was baited with the Schoolmaster with contraceptives (in the published edition the bait was changed to a copy of Casanova's works). The scene closes with the successive appearances of Mordax with his accomplices and of Mollfels with his armed servants; the former are hurrying to kidnap Liddy, the latter to rescue her.

III,6: We see the battle against the villains, Mollfels' rescue of Liddy, her agreement to marry him, and the attempted punishment of Wernthal and Mordax, who escape by jumping into the audience. The Devil, who has fled Hell because it was being scrubbed, is rescued by his young, beautiful grandmother. And, at the end, Grabbe appears carrying a lantern and calls the Schoolmaster a liar. But when the latter tries to keep him out, Liddy concludes the play with the words "Schoolmaster, Schoolmaster, how bitter you are toward the man who wrote you!"

Scherz, Satire is a very entertaining comedy. Its effectiveness on the stage is demonstrated by the fact that it has been performed every year for the last decade in at least one important German theater. In retrospect we may regret that Grabbe did not write more comedies. Ironically, as we read in Alfred Bergmann's *Grabbe in Berichten seiner Zeitgenossen* (p. 121), Grabbe himself once expressed his desire to produce works more suitable for the stage in the field of comedy.

In *Scherz, Satire,* Grabbe uses a characteristically Romantic form, but he does so, not to pay homage to Tieck or Romanticism, but to reject Romantic values. This fact stamps him as a *Weltschmerzler*. It has been shown that poets like Heinrich Heine felt themselves oppressed by the overpowering accomplishments of Romantic poetry, that they could not find a new language of their own because they could not disengage themselves from their Romantic heritage. Thus, Heine writes like a Romantic but undercuts everything he writes with irony and disillusionment. Grabbe, like Heine and, later, Büchner, attacks Romanticism through its own forms.

If the number of comedies in German literature is relatively small, the Romantics are certainly not to blame. Above all, they developed two types of comedy which can be called characteristic for their view of life. On the one hand, there are the so-called fairy-tale comedies, such as Brentano's *Ponce de Leon* and Eichendorff's *Die Freier.* Historically, these comedies were inspired mainly by Shakespeare, particularly such works as *As You Like It,* and, like their model, stressed wit and conceit, puns and absurdity. Philosophically, these comedies fitted well into the entire complex of ideas, notions, and longings which the Romantics found substantiated by fairy tales in general.

On the other hand, Ludwig Tieck produced a number of "fantastic comedies," the best of which, *Der gestiefelte Kater* (1797), was followed by two sequels, *Prinz Zerbino* (1799) and *Die verkehrte Welt* (1798). Once again, Shakespeare furnishes one of the models, for these fantastic comedies share with such works as *A Midsummer Night's Dream* the emphasis on slapstick and other forms of low, visual comedy, fantastic situations and, above all, the overlaying of several strata of action and the resulting disruption of a continuous stage illusion and enveloping atmosphere. It is an irony of literary history that the most effective representatives of both types were written by post-Romantic *Weltschmerzler*, both intent on the destruction of Romantic idealism: Georg Büchner's *Leonce und Lena*, whose fairy-tale atmosphere is like a bubble on the sharp pinpoint of hunger, social injustice, ignorance, and absurdity, and Grabbe's *Scherz, Satire*, which we shall examine first in terms of those very models used by the Romantics, then in terms of Grabbe's different attitude toward them.

The "Jest" in the title of the play reveals the indirect influence of several Romantic inspirations. One of the great discoveries of the Romantics was Aristophanes, whose burlesque and low comedy was cherished for several reasons, the most prominent of which was his breaking of the stage illusion. Friedrich Schlegel justified it in the following way: "This violation [of the rules of the stage] is not a lack of skill but rather calculated caprice, ebullient vivacity, and often does not lessen the effect but rather enhances it."[3] It is obvious from these remarks that the Romantics saw in Aristophanes an intellectual justification for fancy, excess, and boisterousness.

Many of the same qualities also drew them to the *commedia dell'arte* and the German shrovetide farces (carnival plays). The Romantics can also be credited with the renewed interest in the figure of Hanswurst, the German counterpart to the *zani* in the *commedia dell'arte*. Hanswurst had been virtually banished from the stage through the reform efforts of Johann Christoph Gottsched, who was mainly intent on giving the German theater the sophistication of the French. But the Romantics saw Gottsched's reform as an emulation of foreign rules, and it is against just such blind adherence to rules that Tieck's attacks in *Der gestiefelte Kater* are leveled.

Undoubtedly the criticism directed against Gottsched by Lessing and the Romantics was far too harsh. Nevertheless, we see in Tieck's fantastic comedies a justified sally against an artistic malady that cannot be associated with one time or person only. It is against the belief that art can and must be learned and created according to specific rules. Much of the comedy in *Der gestiefelte Kater* is intentionally rough, burlesque, and exaggerated to prove a point learned through the examples of Aristophanes, the *commedia dell'arte,* the German carnival plays, and Shakespeare: that plain fun should not always be sacrificed for the sake of sophistication and well-mannered drama. Grabbe's comedy successfully emulates this Romantic tradition. As a matter of fact, it far exceeds Tieck's comedies in its drastic, earthy qualities.

The Romantics wanted to recapture many elements of popular, folksy comedy, but nowhere did they succeed in creating characters like the Schoolmaster, the Devil, or Mollfels. The Schoolmaster had been a humorous figure from the eighteenth century on, but Grabbe has outdone any possible model in realism and low comedy. As Schneider points out, his Devil is right out of the carnival plays and corresponds to what the village folk would expect him to be. We also note, however, that, divested of virtually all metaphysical qualities, he seems almost like a man who cannot avoid doing evil at every opportunity. Thus Grabbe blends the fantastic and earthy, caprice and realism, imagination and realism. All the characters reflect Grabbe's feeling for, and observation of, lower-class, unsophisticated life, as well as his knowledge of literary and intellectual fads. On a realistic level, we cannot quite believe in the true existence of these characters, yet we are not prepared to assert that there is no such drunken Schoolmaster or no such emancipated young lady as Liddy.

Tieck's fantastic comedies are literary satires. In them he attacks the Enlightenment and its deference to systems, not only by the example of his comedy, but also by direct ridicule. Grabbe's satire is no less recurrent or biting. On the contrary: the truly trivial authors and works suffer in the best of company, for even the major poets of unquestioned greatness, such as Goethe and Schiller, are not spared.

Grabbe also ridicules any system, be it artistic, scientific, or philosophical. Like Tieck, he makes it clear that he does not believe in creating or thinking according to given rules. But there is an important difference between the *Weltschmerzler* and his Romantic model: Tieck wants to shake people's blind reliance on systems in order to evoke their understanding for a higher criterion—the Romantic view of life. In Grabbe's *Scherz, Satire,* however, we have lost the security provided by a substitution for the notions and values under attack. For that reason, Grabbe's satire seems to be far more subjective and personally revealing, but also more nihilistic.

One of the basic tenets of Romanticism is a stated or implied faith in inspiration, and it is in the cause of artistic inspiration that the Romantics satirize systems. Yet even inspiration, seemingly the source not only for Romantic art as a whole but also for the capriciousness of *Scherz, Satire,* comes under fire in Grabbe's caricature of Rattengift, the poet. In Act II, scene 2, Rattengift attempts to compose a sonnet but he has no idea of how to go about it. So he starts to poeticize the idea that he has no idea: "I sat at my table and chewed feathers [quills] like...." After much musing, he finally hits upon the following simile, which he calls "calderonish" (like one by Calderón):[4] "like the lion before the morning dawns chews on the horse, his quick feather." (His train of thought was: what the mane is to the horse, the feather is to the quill.) We would all agree with Rattengift when he concludes that there has never been such a metaphor, but we might raise an eyebrow about his second conclusion: "I am frightened by my own poetic power."

Besides naming names and pointing to the weakness of what he calls the "herring-literature" of the times, Grabbe indulges in quite a bit of parody. The most important example is, perhaps, his travesty of the contemporary love- and adventure-story. Liddy represents the stock heroine of trivial literature: she is attractive, generous (she supports a secret charity), noble (because the charity is kept secret), and wealthy. Iconoclastic as he might have been, Grabbe undoubtedly was less bothered by these aspects of fictional heroines—his own heroines have many of Liddy's virtues—than by the picture of the emancipated woman offered by the female writers he so frequently ridiculed. Liddy is, of course, far from being a man-woman. Yet in the hut, for example, she barricades the door by shoving a table in front of it. The table was too heavy for the men, her uncle and Rattengift, but she moves it alone, as one critic has commented, with the ease of a heavyweight champion.

Grabbe satirizes Liddy's pleasingly feminine qualities indirectly rather than directly. He gives her a suitor who is undoubtedly the ugliest binding in which a noble book has ever been sheathed. Liddy, to be sure, recognizes Mollfels' inner beauty. The fortune-hunting fiancé, Wernthal, was a standard part of the contemporary love story, and unscrupulous plotters like Mordax—though not as violent as he—also grazed the pages of young ladies' reading matter. In such stories, however, the heroine is never forced to forsake her dreams of a handsome rescuer from her difficulties. True to his propensity for radical opposition, however, Grabbe makes Liddy accept a rescuer who is just as ugly on the outside as the villains are on the inside. Even in this supposedly capricious, subjective comedy, Grabbe cannot bring himself to acknowledge a complete correspondence between spiritual and physical being, between ideality and reality.

The "irony" in the title also links Grabbe's comedy with Romanticism, for it calls to mind the so-called Romantic irony and all the associations connected with it. In essence, irony is saying the opposite of what one means, and the Romantics felt they were doing just that when they talked about the material world. Although concerned with the infinite, spiritual, divine side of existence, the Romantics could only use the finite, the material, the secular side. One of the reasons why the Romantic writers were so extravagant in their praise of Aristophanes, the *commedia dell'arte* and other dramatic forms that break the illusion of causal reality on the stage was because they found that the infinite mind of the author was implying its freedom from the shackles of the cause-effect relationships of the finite, material world. Brentano calls such a technique "falling out of the piece." What such ironic breaking of the illusion really means is "falling out of the world," for it asserts the primacy of the free spirit, the ability of the artist to drop out of the world he himself created and to say: I have put these characters in this or that circumstance, but I can change them at will. The Romanticists stress, therefore, the irreality of the physical world. How often, for example, does Eichendorff speak of the "spectacle of life" (*Schauspiel des Lebens*). This life and this world seem to be only the props on a stage, behind which lies the infinite, ideal, divine, and true "reality."

Grabbe likewise shatters the illusion of the stage events when Mordax and Wernthal simply "drop out of the piece" and thereby escape their punishment. Another typically Romantic technique is the breaking of the illusion by the appearance of the author himself, a technique Grabbe employs at the end of his play. But in both cases, there is a bitterness that belies the Romantic optimism of a free spirit. Mordax and Wernthal escape from the reality of responsibility, and their actions are not dissimilar to the "dropping out" that Leonce, Lena, and Valerio commit in Büchner's comedy. Such examples represent flights from oppressive reality, not an assertion of spiritual freedom. We must remember that Tieck, when his characters (such as "Der blonde Eckbert") are confronted with moral responsibility, does not allow them so easy an escape. The figurative escape from physical reality is possible for the Romantic because it lies in a state of mind he has attained. Stressing the captivity of the mind, the *Weltschmerzler* Grabbe and, later, Büchner make the escape physical and, therefore, absurdly impossible. One of the most notable lines in *Hannibal* will be the protagonist's statement: "Yes, we won't fall out of the world. We're in it once and for all" (III, 153). In effect, however, this is only a succinct reiteration of the thought already expressed by Gothland: man's thoughts are eagles, but he remains stuck in the mud.

There is, in addition, no triumph in Grabbe's rupture of the illusion through his own appearance at the conclusion; for he is powerless against the Schoolmaster, who has just called him "the cursed Grabbe, or, as one should really call him, the pigmy crab, the author of this piece! He is as stupid as a crowbar, insults all writers and isn't worth anything himself, has disjointed legs, crossed eyes and an insipid monkey face." Grabbe returns these insults by calling the Schoolmaster a liar, but he does not threaten the existence of his own creation. Liddy speaks the last word when she tells the Schoolmaster not to be so embittered toward the man who created him. Grabbe seems to have lost control over his figures and cannot simply assert his artistic freedom over them, as a Romantic writer might have done. There is a veiled implication that, although Grabbe wrote the comedy, it has a real existence, and that the play is indeed the real world, as bizarre as this may seem.

For the Romantic, the play is just a play, but so is the world around us. The theme of the "world as a play" also occurs in Grabbe's comedy, but the accents have been radically shifted. So important is the theme that Grabbe, as Benno von Wiese points out, had to make this comedy a literary satire. In a letter, Grabbe singled out the conversation, in Act II, scene 2, between the Devil and Rattengift as being particularly significant. In this dialogue, the Devil answers Rattengift's question about the nature of the world: "Then I want to tell you that this embodiment of the universe that you honor with the name 'world,' is nothing more than a mediocre comedy which a beardless, brash young angel—who lives in the orderly world incomprehensible for man and, if I'm not mistaken, is still in his last year of secondary school—scribbled down during his school vacation." And when Rattengift asks about Hell, which is also in the world, he receives the following answer: "Hell is the ironic part of the piece, and as is usually the case, turned out better for the twelfth-grader than Heaven, which is supposed to be merely the serene part of the piece." Thus, Heaven and Hell are only parts of the same mediocre comedy as life. There may be a realm in which the boy angel exists, but we know nothing about it.

The Romantics felt that their sense for the irony of existence was proof enough for the existence of Heaven and of the divine. Grabbe, however, equates Hell with irony. Heaven is *merely* the serene part. Thus, the irony is, itself, more important and accessible than what it should imply. The Romantic idealist tried to overcome the irony of a finite world as an expression of the infinite, but Grabbe, the *Weltschmerzler,* could not reconcile himself with the existence of this irony. God is not mentioned in *Scherz, Satire,* but the Devil, the representative of the ironic, appears in the play because Grabbe is sure only of the irony, not of what it signifies. For him, "irony" is only a rhetorical term, and, we may assume, so are "Heaven" and "Hell"—a view that will be substantiated in *Don Juan und Faust.* The words exist, but, Grabbe seems to ask, do the things they supposedly represent? We recall the powerlessness of the dramatist Grabbe at the end of the comedy: once the characters he had created existed, he could change nothing, even though they were only the products of his imagination. The threat of man's own thoughts, words, and systems to dominate him will recur as a problem in many of his later dramas.

The "deeper significance" promised by the title of the play is seen by most critics in the above passage describing the world as a mediocre comedy. With few exceptions, they imply that such significance is only tacked on. Actually, however, the "significance" is not separable from the "jest," "satire," and "irony." That is to say, the deeper significance is joined, not by a disjunctive, but by a conjunctive "and," with those elements that produce the laughter. The deeper significance lies, therefore, in the laughter. Georg Büchner once said that he laughed about man, not because of the how he is what he is, but rather because he is a man. Grabbe's laughter has similar origins. In a letter, Grabbe refers to the "laughter of desperation" (*Lachen der Verzweiflung*) in *Scherz, Satire* (V, 309). If the world is really as absurd as is implied by his comedy, this is the only kind of laughter it could evoke.

We recall, moreover, Gothland's statement that "desperation is the only true worship of God" (I, 83). How close *Gothland* and *Scherz, Satire* are related to one another is pointed out by Grabbe himself in his letter to Kettembeil of June 1, 1827: "*Gothland* is followed by the comedy, which, to be sure, stems from the same basic views, but in its outwardly frantically comic appearance [is] a complete contrast to the tragic *Gothland*" (V, 278). We have already noted that contrast and opposition characterized Grabbe's personality and work. Many years later, Büchner, another poet torn between extremes, will also write a comedy as the reverse side of his tragedy *Dantons Tod*.[5] Grabbe's repetition of motifs, themes, and images in *Scherz, Satire* makes it clear that he anticipates such a complementary view of the same problem. One can only ask, however: To what extent are the tragic and comic sides really separable?[6] What links *Scherz, Satire* to *Gothland* and how closely?

In *Scherz, Satire,* as in *Gothland,* the Devil appears, although this time under his own name. But here, too, he is a physical anomaly. Once again, the Devil attacks man's pretensions to knowledge of the infinite. But even more significance can be attributed to the fact that he is the protagonist of a comedy which, as Joachim Kaiser says, destroys our faith in all categories of human perception. He tells us about a realm that lies beyond man's comprehension. And when the scientists refuse to accept his existence because their system does not allow for a devil, we have living proof that man cannot, and will not, accept the obvious because he is so entangled in his own systems. Like Berdoa, the Devil functions as a grotesque catalyst in the revelation of man's inability to understand the world about him and of man's own tendency to deceive himself.

The basic image in *Scherz, Satire* is that of the theater and the world as a comedy. That Grabbe's comedy is not merely intended to be good, plain fun is obvious in the scene in which Mordax kills the journeymen tailors. These murders belong to the madhouse atmosphere which is symptomatic of a world that has become an absurd comedy, an atmosphere that is characteristic of modern plays like Peter Weiss's *Marat/de Sade* or Friedrich Dürrenmatt's *Physiker*. But these wanton murders evoke memories of *Gothland*. Directing that the murders in *Scherz, Satire* be carried out in pantomime, Grabbe deprives them of some of their seriousness—that the well-mannered murderer takes out a napkin does not really increase the horror either—and, at the same time, shows how pointless they are. The murder of journeymen tailors under such circumstances is simply grotesque. But was not the slaughter in *Gothland* almost too horrible to be real? In *Scherz, Satire* the pointlessness is shown; in *Gothland* it is implied. Berdoa is serious in his contempt for human life, an attitude later assumed by Gothland. The Devil in *Scherz, Satire* says that murderers are laughed at in Hell for bothering to take a human life. His statement assumes, in retrospect, the proportions of a comic substantiation of Berdoa's view, which we have already described as constituting a Mephistophelean ethic.

In *Scherz, Satire*, as in *Gothland*, personal heroism represents one of the main themes. But in the former it is parodied through the characters of Liddy and Mollfels.

In both plays, sex, like murder and heroism, appears as a reaction against the pallor, hypocrisy, and sentimentality of the *Biedermeier*. The comic variation occurs in *Scherz, Satire* when the Devil is caught in the cage because of his lasciviousness. In *Gothland*, of course, Berdoa uses sex to entice the Duke's son from both his father and the way of idealism: Carl Anton Piper shows in detail how Grabbe, through the figure of Gustav, parodies both the style and the content of Klopstock's love poetry. A similar contempt for woman's virtues and sentimental love links the comic Devil with Berdoa. Even though *Scherz, Satire* seems to conclude with a triumph of just such sentimentalized attraction, the forthcoming marriage between Liddy and Mollfels impresses us as but little less grotesque than the marriage, in J. M. R. Lenz's *Hofmeister,* between the self-emasculated Läuffer and Lise. In his comedy, Grabbe, like Lenz fifty years earlier, attacks the influence of sentimental love stories on young ladies as well as the influence of the contemporary emancipation movements, but with more cynicism than moral indignation.

The fate tragedies, which, as we have seen, play such a significant role in Grabbe's treatment of the Swedish Duke's tragedy, are parodied in *Scherz, Satire.* Mollfels tells Liddy that he has written a "tasteless tragedy" whose content he must relate (I, 251-52). Instead of Fate, he lets the "goddess of the anti-fatalists, boredom," reign. During Grabbe's time, the word "boredom" was laden with meaning, particularly for the *Weltschmerzler.* Not until he creates his Don Juan does Grabbe find the right vehicle for treating this concept in depth. In *Scherz, Satire,* however, its significance as a renunciation of fate, that is, of a universal plan, is already suggested. We have already seen that Gothland dies in a state of complete apathy; through Mollfels and his unrequited love we hear an absurdly comic glorification of boredom as symptomatic of the unobtainable, ideal love. Mollfel's "tragedy" represents the comic counterpart to Gothland's tragic inability to find any principle of good in world history.

Taken together, *Gothland* and *Scherz, Satire* present a tragicomic world of absurdity, a world of moral and physical chaos, in which ideal meaning cannot be found. Later interpretations will demonstrate how Grabbe brings the tragic and comic elements increasingly closer to each other, until he arrives at one of his most important modes of expression: the tragicomedy. In *Hannibal,* which shows true mastery of this genre, Scipio the Elder says, "What is tragic is also amusing, and vice versa. For I have, after all, often laughed in tragedies and have almost been moved in comedies" (III, 104). Throughout his career, Grabbe's propensity for the tragicomic will be inseparably tied, as in *Gothland* and its comic counterpart, with the problem of fate. Over and over again we shall see how Grabbe attempts to resolve the conflict between his belief in a personal fate and a meaningless, chaotic world that seems to reveal no timeless principles as a guiding force.

Touching on the fate problem represents about the only redeeming feature of *Nannette und Maria.* It is certainly the only feature in this rather banal work that links it with the rest of Grabbe's dramas.

III Nannette und Maria

Act I, scene 1: The play opens on a pastoral scene. Count Leonardo appears and is immediately joined by Nannette and several girls who dance and sing. The girls soon leave, and Leonardo, now alone with Nannette, declares his love for her. At first reticent to admit her attraction to him, she finally acknowledges her love. She must return, she says, to her father, "the old, righteous [*bieder*] nobleman Pietro." Such a description in a play by Grabbe suggests, of course, more irony than sincerity. The first scene of this "moving" verse play ends with Leonardo's affirmation of uncontrolled love. Grabbe shows that he can write good verse in *Gothland* and *Marius und Sulla.* But the inadequacy of his poetry in this play reveals how dependent his poetic powers were on the subject matter: here he was forced to express ideas for which he had already shown great contempt, and his verses alternate between banality and inappropriateness.

I,2: In the country home of Marchese Alfredi. A conversation between Alfredi and his sister Maria deals with how Alfredi has insulted a lady because she had been unjust to Maria, for whom he would do anything. Deceived by his fiancée and persecuted by his mother, Alfredi admits his hatred of all other women. The main conflict in the drama is revealed in Maria's relationship to Leonardo, whom she loves, but who does not love her. Leonardo, with whom she was betrothed in childhood, comes to free her from their engagement. She returns his ring to him.

II,1: Pietro notices the change in his daughter. Soon Leonardo enters and asks for Nannette's hand. Pietro gives his permission.
II,2: In Alfredi's residence, where he asks his sister what is wrong with her. Despite her denial, Alfredi suspects that Leonardo has insulted her.

II,3: Leonardo and Nannette are at a pastor's home in the mountains. The pastor, who has been visiting a sick person, returns and extols his idyllic existence in the forest. II,4: On a green hill, accompanied by the typically Romantic "sounds of a hunting horn out of the distance." (Incidentally, the recounting of such details shows not only how far Grabbe was willing to prostitute himself to contemporary taste and to what he thought Tieck might like; it also shows how superficial he considered contemporary drama. The inclusion of an idyllic setting, nobility, a pastor, a righteous noble father, and hunting horns is all that he considered necessary for success.) The final scene of the act concludes with more raptures on idyllic pleasures and Nannette's expression of her anxiety to Leonardo about their coming marriage. In later dramas, Grabbe's praise of the idyllic sounds somewhat more convincing, but only as an unobtainable release from a more typically Grabbean world of political chaos.

III,1: We return to Alfredi's country palace. Maria's maid tells her that Leonardo has married Nannette. Maria is desperate and disappointed.

III,2: Pietro, Leonardo and Nannette are in a pavilion in Leonardo's park. Maria enters and watches the festivities: the toasts to the marriage are, for her, toasts to her death. In a similar scene in *Don Juan und Faust,* the former, cynical, and witty, will also listen to, and contemptuously comment on, a conventional declaration of love—but how much more convincing is his monologue! Seen by Leonardo, Maria claims that she has merely been walking with Lenore, her maid, who, when she faints, carries her away. Alfredi enters demanding revenge for Maria, whom he has seen on a hill and believed to be dying. From the ring on Nannette's finger, he sees that she is married to Leonardo. Torn between hatred and fascination with her beauty, he hits her. She dies and Alfredi leaves. Maria arrives and discovers her body. When Leonardo and Pietro return, the former, believing that Maria has killed his wife, stabs her. Alfredi returns. He tells Leonardo that he has killed Nannette, but that Maria has accepted the blame in order to die by Leonardo's hand. Alfredi and Leonardo duel and wound each other. A reconciliation between them over Maria's body closes this sentimental tragedy, with which Grabbe—as he states in his foreword—tried to reconcile the readers who found *Goth-land* repulsive.

The play seems like an unintentional parody of the problems treated in *Gothland*: Alfredi's being torn between love and hate (cf. Berdoa's doctrine of great love and great hate), the misinterpretation of appearances (Gothland also believes that a murder had taken place where there had been none), the duel between friends. (Gothland, of course, fights his own brother, but these two are almost like brothers.) *Scherz, Satire* is an intentional, seriously comic parody of *Gothland* with a truly deeper significance. *Nannette und Maria* is simply, like Mollfels' nose, "flat as a story by Karoline Pichler" (a feminine novelist satirized in *Scherz, Satire*). In trying to give his contemporaries what they wanted, Grabbe betrayed himself and his talent (he later referred to this play as his "little whore").

As a play, *Gothland* is too long for a stage production. *Scherz, Satire* has the proper length but has no real successor in Grabbe's later production. *Nannette und Maria* is scarcely worth staging. In the fourth of the *Dramatische Dichtungen, Marius und Sulla,* the length would, once again, present a prospective theater with nearly insurmountable problems. But in terms of the stage, *Marius* is unique among the four, for here Grabbe begins to develop some of the innovations that will make his later historical dramas some of the great experiments in German theatrical history. In this sense, *Marius* seems, despite its fragmentary character, more mature than any of the other serious dramas in the collection. Such maturity stems undoubtedly from the fact that the published drama represents a complete revision of the first version (the second, printed version of *Scherz, Satire* differs from the first mainly in certain allusions and in the vocabulary).[7]

IV Marius und Sulla: *A Tragedy in Five Acts*

In his foreword to this drama, Grabbe states that he is submitting this fragment to the public for its judgment as to whether it should be completed.

Act I, scene 1: Near Carthage's ruins, a fisher, his wife, and his son discuss Cajus Marius' presence there after his expulsion from Rome by Cornelius Sulla (in 88 B.C.). Marius himself appears with his followers. Completely exhausted, they think that all is lost until Marius' son, Marius the Younger, arrives with the news that Cinna, who has revolted against Octavius and Rome, is calling for Marius' return. The thought of his return to Rome gives the old man, six times a consul, new strength.

I,2: In his camp Mithridates is developing immunity to poison by taking small doses. He is preparing for battle with Sulla on the next morning. I,3: Sulla's camp. In a conversation with Kaphis, a Greek, Sulla learns that Octavius has driven Cinna out of Rome but that he is awaiting Marius and gaining support from the mobs. I,4: The battle between Mithridates and Sulla. Although the latter is victorious, his thoughts are focused on Marius.

I,5: The peace between Sulla and Mithridates is the subject of this scene. Because civil war is threatening Rome, Sulla must allow his conquered opponent to keep Pontus, but Mithridates, who admits that he wants to help the Romans destroy each other, gives Sulla two hundred ships instead of the seventy demanded. Grabbe's advance over *Gothland* to a truly historical drama, despite all of the liberties he takes with the facts of history, is obvious: the characters and forces are moving the action in terms of historic consideration of power and politics, not merely personal emotions.

II,1: Cinna's camp. Sertorius warns Cinna that his rabble is not to be trusted. Throughout the play, Grabbe shows a striking ability to re-create the atmosphere of deception, conspiracy, and counterconspiracy that dominated the "civilized" world of the time. Cinna thinks that he can use Marius for his own purposes to unite the army. Marius returns and welcomes his old soldiers whose fanatical loyalty contrasts sharply with the attitude of the other soldiers. But Marius' advanced age and his appearance surprise Cinna. While Marius is giving the sign to begin the reconquest of Rome, Cinna and Sertorius are already planning for a possible fight against Marius.

II,2: This session of the Senate in Rome is the subject of one of Grabbe's best scenes. The tribunes, Saturninus and Flavius, hinder the work of the Senate because they demand more for the people. They want land to be distributed before helping to defend Rome. The Senate we see here is caught in complacency and stifling tradition. Word arrives that the army has been defeated and that the frightened public has begun to riot. When the tribunes try to use their veto against surrender, they are overridden by the patricians. The tribunes are forced to flee and are pursued as traitors by the mob. After arguing among themselves, the patricians under Octavius' leadership leave to surrender the city to Marius.

II,3: A mob that is plundering Rome attacks the palace of Scaevola. Through demagoguery Saturninus is able to gain control of this mob. One of Grabbe's most brilliant creations—he has no counterpart in history—Saturninus is a cynical opportunist contemptuous of the very people who follow him. Yet when Saturninus tries to lead the mob against the soldiers of Crassus the Elder, they flee. Saturninus escapes, but Crassus captures Flavius and prepares to defend the city until Sulla's return. News spreads of Marius' and Cinna's victories. Crassus still wants to execute Flavius, but the execution of a tribune would give Marius an excuse to plunder. Badly wounded, Octavius returns and drops dead. The senators set out to surrender to Marius. Crassus, who still wants to resist, is stabbed by Saturninus. The mob, following Saturninus and crying Marius' name, now attacks and kills Scaevola.

II,4: Marius prepares to enter the city. He gives orders to spare no one because of the insults against his name. The ambassadors who come to surrender the city to Marius are largely ignored by him, who then leads his troops into the city. The plots of Act II, scenes 5, 6, and 7 are described by Grabbe. The fifth scene is supposed to show the rioting and bloodshed caused first by the mob, then by Marius and his troops. The sixth scene treats the suicide of Merula, Pontifex Maximus. Tribute is brought Marius, who soon hears, however, that Sulla has landed in Italy. He orders the arrest of Metella, Sulla's wife, who is still living in Rome. The seventh scene opens in Metella's room. At first she refuses to hide from Marius, but when she sees Marius' legions leaving to fight Sulla, she flees to join her husband.

III,1: Part of the dialogue in this scene is printed as such, but the rest is paraphrased and the action is described as it would ultimately have been written. The scene opens with a speech by Sulla on "fortune." Marius is then reunited with Metella, who tells him about the bloodbath in Rome. Sulla's next speech is called by Grabbe the "transition": "The mob is mistaken, if it believes I have no feelings because I have controlled them. Oh, they are all the more terrible the more they obey me. I made them into tame pets; they lick my clothes with fear and flattery, but woe to him on whom I set them [like animals]." The rest of the scene consists mainly of Grabbe's description of Sulla's character, particularly his "humor," which is increasing with each horror scene. In this observation we see how Grabbe intended to reinforce the tragicomic aspects, and we sense his growing recognition of them as his forte. If Gothland's was a laughter of desperation, Sulla's is one of cruelty.

III,2: Consisting partly of Grabbe's own account, this scene deals with Cinna's and Sertorius' plot to massacre the Marius followers and abandon Marius to his fate. Cinna tries to persuade Marius to join him in an attack on Sulla, but the old man finds that it is still too early. The scene concludes with festivities that should, according to Grabbe, prove that Marius has not lost his powers as a leader. To the reader, however, it becomes increasingly clear that this torso of a drama, if Grabbe had carried out everything he sketched in, would have become a work of enormous length. Although Grabbe seldom shows any apprehension regarding the endurance of his audiences, we suspect that he may not have wanted to finish the drama because it would have exceeded *Gothland* in size. On the other hand, we understand his reluctance to delete any of the above, mainly because he had already accomplished a remarkable condensation of gigantic temporal and spatial relationships. Grabbe planned the third, concluding scene as a camp scene revealing the devotion of Marius' followers to their leader and their hatred of Sulla.

IV. The remaining events exist only as described by Grabbe. Marius has just mounted his horse when he suddenly falls dead. Refusing to halt the attack, his son proclaims himself his father's successor. The army marches off with Marius' body. In his camp, Sulla waits for news of his plot against Cinna, whose camp is not far away. Under the pretext of negotiations, Sulla has sent ambassadors whose real purpose it is to bribe Cinna's army to desert its leader. He receives news that Cinna has been murdered by his generals and that his army has dispersed or is about to join his own. Sulla then learns of Marius' death. Sulla, we are told, excels in a long discussion by both his comprehension of the problems and by his ruthlessness: in particular, he says that Rome is so sick that much blood must be let to restore its full health. When word reaches his camp that young Marius is approaching with a growing army, numerically superior to Sulla's own, the latter discounts the advice to retreat. He attacks and triumphs. Soon the rumor of young Marius' death arises.

In the third scene, we learn that the remnants of Marius' army have fled to Pontius Telesinus, the leader of the Sammites, who avows his hatred of Rome. It becomes known that Sulla has pledged to kill to a man everyone who has borne arms against him. He has all of the Praenestines, who revolted against him, killed, but quickly overcomes his initial horror about the act. Hearing of Telesinus' preparations for war, Sulla recognizes the danger of his opponents' reaching Rome first. The fourth scene would have been a characterization of Telesinus, who plans only to use Marius' followers in order to conquer Rome. He breaks camp to march against Sulla and the Romans. Shouting that Sulla is dead, Telesinus' army enters Rome. Telesinus now reveals his true face and has the followers of Marius slaughtered. Sulla arrives, however, and after a fierce battle, Telesinus' army flees.

V: Sulla comes to Rome and, despite the pleas of the Senate and the populace, begins the proscriptions. Saturninus, the cynical but successful demagogue, also tries his wiles on Sulla, but the latter sees through him and has him executed. In the last scene, episodes of terror in the city show the executions, which last for weeks. We realize, however, that this bloodletting has little in common with the numerous slaughters in *Gothland*. Saturninus, Telesinus, and the others have already set the precedent sufficiently for us to associate wholesale murder with the cruel times. Sulla sees the complete elimination of his enemies as the only way of restoring permanent order to the Roman Empire, which has been torn so long by internal strife. This corresponds to Sulla's character and his cold logic, and it makes the conclusion of the play all the more startling.

Sulla is named dictator, and the city prepares for his triumphant march through the streets. Now master of the world, Sulla himself appears with a laurel wreath, views the power surrounding him and says, "All of this is useless to me. I don't need it. I have done my part, and from now on, being myself is enough." He renounces all his power and leaves with his wife for Cumae, where he will live in peace and solitude. If Grabbe had finished the play without giving any more insights than he did in the prose descriptions of Sulla, we would have been left with a significant problem: was he, despite his inhuman actions which are so readily acceptable in their historical context, basically altruistic? Was he only a patriot wanting to restore order and knowing the only means by which order could be restored? Or is the end only the inevitable conclusion for a totally logical mind: even for one who incontestably owns all of it, the world is not really worth the trouble of possession.

Grabbe has appended a footnote to the play which, together with some of his other remarks, helps us to understand his intentions. His footnote begins: "The poet is primarily obligated to decipher the true spirit of history. As long as he does not violate this [spirit], literal historical accuracy need not be essential for him. The author of *Marius und Sulla* has, to be sure, sought to adhere more exactly to history than is the preponderance of other historical dramatists, and yet has had to transpose entire years. If the reader hears a *false note* [*Mißklang*] —that is a mistake."

In the history of German literature, Grabbe is known primarily as the author of historical dramas. Benno von Wiese, in his book *Die deutsche Tragödie von Lessing bis Hebbel*, shows that Grabbe's unique contribution to this genre lies in his ability to make history come to life. The above quotation, together with the following notions expressed by Grabbe, represents, according to Wolfgang Hegele, almost the "theoretical foundation for the future form of Grabbe's historical dramas" (p. 173). Two of the other quotations stem from "Concerning the Shakespeare-Mania":

But from the poet, as soon as he dramatizes history, I also demand a dramatic, concentric treatment which reproduces the idea of history. Schiller strove for this, and the healthy, German mind directed him: none of his historical plays is without a dramatic center and without a concentric idea.

The German people want as much simplicity and clarity as possible in language, structure and plot.

With great attention to the technical detail in Grabbe's histories, especially in his scenic method of presentation, Hegele makes a convincing case for Grabbe's skill as a dramatist and, above all, for the assertion that the mass scenes in these dramas are carefully composed with a view toward incorporating the "spirit" of the time presented.

The first version of *Marius*, written around 1823, is, in its mass scenes, largely indebted to Shakespeare. But the second version, stemming, as it does, from the time of Grabbe's critical essay on Shakespeare and Shakespearianism, introduces a new, truly original technique. The new technique will present the "spirit" and the idea of history, something that Grabbe felt was often missing in Shakespeare's chronicles.

Although he cites Schiller as a model preferable to Shakespeare, we may not, as Hegele points out, equate Grabbe's "idea of history" with the "concentric idea" he praises in Schiller's work. Schiller, like Goethe, is concerned with the generally humane, the universal and timeless idea inherent in a historical situation. Grabbe restricts himself to the specific historical idea in a specific period. We have already seen how unable he was to raise Gothland's problem successfully to an ontological level without losing the historical flavor of the piece. The later historical dramas, like *Marius,* carry out this program because Grabbe renounces, except by tone and implication, the revelation of universal truths and ideas in history.

Nor may we view the "spirit" intended by Grabbe as a reflection of Hegelianism. For Grabbe, the "spirit" need not be of rational or logical origin, nor need it lead to a logical resolution. It exists rather for its own sake. There is no Hegelian synthesis of the two conflicting forces or ideas incorporated by Marius and Sulla, and any future developments are rendered impossible by Sulla's abdication.

Correctly or incorrectly, Friedrich Hebbel has been called "Hegelian" because his dramas, for example, *Agnes Bernauer,* end on the very conciliatory, progressive note absent from Grabbe's plays. Hebbel's dramas portray the conflict of two historical forces, out of which a third, higher force must evolve. In short, Hebbel's Agnes Bernauer and the other characters of that play are caught up in history as necessarily evolving. Although Sulla's actions seem to be "necessary," their necessity stems from his own recognition of the actual historical situation, its demands and the climate, not from a universal, superpersonal plan, of which he is only a part. Sulla has, at the end of the play, restored a previous situation; he has not reached a new, higher plateau.

Like Gothland, all of Grabbe's historical characters live for the "moment," and the "spirit" that pervades his histories is created by the "facts" devoid of all abstract, metaphysical principles implying knowledge beyond the present moment. Not only does such a "spirit" imply the negation of progress and development; in Grabbe's works it becomes more and more commensurate with history seen as a senseless cycle into which man "reads the good." Grabbe would certainly concede that after Sulla or any other person the world is never again completely the same as before. But there is no indication that it is really better or worse.

Grabbe praises his mass scenes (V, 310), and rightfully so. Several of them effectively evoke the atmosphere and spirit of the times. But they are not merely naturalistic re-creations of details. There is an undercurrent of cynicism in them that anticipates the scenes in Grabbe's great historical dramas on Napoleon and Hannibal. To achieve his own, individual "tone" Grabbe uses two techniques: a sort of caricatured realism and a so-called commentary technique.

Portraying a historical epoch in all its breadth is accomplished in *Marius und Sulla* by the use of representative types from different classes, professions, and opinions. We not only hear about the patricians and the masses, the generals and the politicians, the wealthy and the poor, the brave and the cowardly, the loyal and the perfidious—we actually see them portrayed through individual representatives. Thus a principle of selectivity becomes obvious in the scenes which seem almost chaotic in their abundance of characters. But—and this is one of Grabbe's most significant achievements—these characters are not merely the standard bearers of abstract ideas. By and large they all have dimension. At the same time, we note that Grabbe's types tend toward caricature. If he had been writing in the twentieth century, one might have expected from him caricatured realism of the type we encounter in Georg Grosz's drawings or in the mass scenes used by many Expressionists. No better example of this quality in Grabbe's first truly historical play can be found than in Saturninus, who also represents the second technique, the "commentary technique."

Some critics, Max Spalter, for example, view Saturninus as being superfluous to the plot. This point could be conceded as far as the main plot is concerned, but Saturninus is nevertheless absolutely essential for the drama as a whole. In his prose paraphrase of the action in Act II, scene 5, Grabbe writes: "It becomes more and more obvious in the progress of the work that the Roman world no longer has a solid foundation either on earth nor in religion and that, if it is not going to fall apart, only despotism can hold it together. For that reason men like Marius and Sulla appear and become what they have become" (I, 388). More than any other character, Saturninus both personifies, and comments on, this lack of foundation. Through him we see and hear how fickle the masses are, how susceptible they are to a demagogue, and how they will abandon their leader as soon as he no longer has the physical power to force obedience. These times are made for an opportunist, and Saturninus is one. These are times in which the voices of rationality and moderation are drowned out, the times of fear, irrationality, and injustice, all of which Saturninus uses to his own advantage. A forerunner of Jouve, the old revolutionary in *Napoleon,* Saturninus shows us as well, however, that the man who leads the masses against their exploiters does not do so out of idealism or a love of humanity. Saturninus reveals a contempt for humanity that, until now, had been approached only by Berdoa.

As much as is new in *Marius und Sulla,* many of the problems from the other plays recur here. The technical innovations, in many cases, only serve basic attitudes that have changed but little since *Gothland.* Nevertheless, Grabbe has also developed new variations on some of his fundamental ideas.

Gothland is a man torn apart (*zerrissen*) by the inner conflict between his ideals and reality. Much of what makes the Swedish Duke a *Weltschmerzler* is transferred to Marius. Hegele (p. 185), Schneider (p. 155), Siefert (p. 45), and others discern in Marius a similarly pessimistic view of ideals and the disappointment of a man of feeling (*Gefühlsmensch*). It is obvious that Marius has ideals never known to Saturninus and, for that reason, is torn apart by the schism he feels between these ideals and his own insignificance. He says: "Even I am growing old: time is my illness. . . . If I think about the progress of the Roman Empire and my life, . . . then the arch of heaven seems to me almost the inside of a gigantic skull and we are its whims [*Grillen*].—I am one [of those whims] that it, as much as I may resist, is about to forget" (I, 396). Once again "time" represents the almighty principle of the world. The image of man as only a "whim" is, of course, an extension of Gothland's image of man's own thoughts as "eagles" in his skull. In showing man as the caprice of a perhaps malicious power, it also anticipates several passages in Büchner's *Dantons Tod.*

Grabbe has, however, gone one step further: he has not only made Marius a divided man; he has also objectified this division of human nature by the creation of dual heroes. One can almost say that Sulla incorporates the very qualities that are incomplete in, and by their absence cause the suffering of, Marius. In his letter of May 4, 1827, Grabbe writes to Kettembeil: "My protracted operation of pouring understanding, like nitric acid, on my feeling seems to be reaching its end: understanding has been poured out and feeling is demolished" (V, 270). And in his review of the *Dramatische Dichtungen,* Grabbe concludes: "One senses in his works only the ruins of a destroyed subjectivity" (V, 310). From these statements, we may deduce Grabbe's own belief that rationality is the only solution for a man of feeling and that he had tried to show the destruction of subjective feelings in his first dramas. If such is indeed the case, then Sulla must represent Grabbe's ideal, as opposed to Gothland and Marius, with whom he associates his own character. Grabbe substantiates this conjecture in his letter of July 12, 1827 to Kettembeil: "Sincerely, Sulla himself is going to be a highly unusual fellow: he is supposed to become my *ideal* (don't forget, my ideal, for otherwise it would be very little") (V, 288). As Hegele shows (p. 183), Grabbe changes the historical Sulla, who was troubled, throughout his career, by his conscience, into what we would today call a "thinking machine." He personifies complete objectivity and logic. But such an ideal is understandable only from the standpoint of the problems evoked by Gothland and Marius, the *Weltschmerzler.*

Sulla follows his logical view of events without compunction. Ironically, however, such a man is not free. Grabbe, as a person, might have supposed Sulla to be his ideal because he is free of moral restrictions and, consequently, feels no guilt. But, as a dramatist and historian, Grabbe realized that Sulla has perhaps even less freedom than those ruled by their emotions. He is ruled by logic, to be sure, but his logical solution to problems depends on events and circumstances. His mind will allow him no action except the necessary one. Today we would say that he has the same emotional freedom from, but intellectual dependence on, given facts as a computer. Perhaps for that very reason he withdraws from the world of politics to become "himself," to become an individual. More and more Grabbe emphasizes the necessity for being an individual as well as the restrictions of the world and the human mind, its thoughts and systems, on such individuality. In fact, his stress on individuality, on the "revolution of the individual," stamps Grabbe as a forerunner of the Expressionists, the twentieth-century rebels against a technological society.

When we view Marius and Sulla as two types, however, we should not forget Grabbe's skill in presenting them as historical figures, not as mere abstractions of certain human characteristics. In his description of the empire at that time (I, 388), Grabbe makes it clear that he envisions the evolution of such types as symptomatic of the times. If the times had not been conducive to their formation, such types would not have come to the forefront, nor would their characteristics, particularly Sulla's relentless cruelty, have been developed to the extreme. Most critics agree that Marius and Sulla do not develop as individuals but that the times develop them into what they are. We see, for example, how far they are removed from the characters in Schiller's *Maria Stuart*, in which the heroine's fate is ultimately decided by her encounter with Elizabeth. Schiller creates this encounter contrary to historical fact. In making it the turning point of Mary's fate, he leaves us with a belief in man's ability to assert his personality, to determine his actions, and to reveal his own character. Grabbe does not allow Marius and Sulla such an encounter. Their characters are formed not through conflict with other characters but through circumstances beyond them or any other individual.

The only thing linking Marius and Sulla is fate. Marius says in desperation: "Iron necessity of fate! Why did I have to be born with him in the same century? No one could challenge me, if only he, only he did not stand in my way" (I, 396). It is the paradox of history, at least in Grabbe's dramas, that fate, like history, makes a man great yet causes his downfall. But fate has nothing to do with any force beyond the historical one. And even the place in this world to which history has brought a man is meaningless to the completely logical person with a view for the makeup of historical forces. As such a logical person, Sulla sees no point in power. Although he does not directly say so, his contempt for the world, manifested by his renunciation of its riches and might, imparts, no less than the Devil's statement in *Scherz, Satire,* Grabbe's continued belief that the world is only a "mediocre comedy." There is, therefore, no radical departure from the values underlying the earlier dramas. The second version of *Marius und Sulla* distinguishes itself mainly through a discernible maturation of Grabbe's views because he has shown his ability to link them to the tangible world of historical fact.

CHAPTER 3

The Works of Transition

I Don Juan und Faust. *A Tragedy in Four Acts*

ACT I, Scene 1: Rome, near the Spanish embassy. In answer to his questions, Don Juan is told by his servant Leporello that Donna Anna is with her father Don Gusman, the former Spanish governor and present ambassador. Anna is engaged to Don Octavio. In front of Don Gusman's palace, Don Juan stages a mock combat with Leporello, who flees when the household is aroused. Don Juan introduces himself and plays on their sentiments by emphasizing his love of Spain. He explains the noise created by his fight with Leporello as a fight with, and repulsion of, Faust, who supposedly wanted to kidnap Donna Anna. The governor, as Grabbe calls Don Gusman, invites Juan to his daughter's wedding, and then, together with Don Octavio, sets out in pursuit of Faust.

After gloating over sending his irate countrymen after Faust, Don Juan asks Leporello whether he has made the acquaintance of Donna Anna's chambermaid, Lisette, and found out where her mistress's room is. As it turns out, Leporello, who has passed himself off as a count, has had quite a notable success with her: he wakes the maid with a song and learns that Donna Anna will be walking in the garden the next morning.

I,2: Faust's room in Rome is seen. At the end of a long monologue, Faust conjures up the Devil, who appears as a middle-aged knight, dressed in the style of the sixteenth century, but all in black. In return for the Black Knight's promise to show him how he could have found happiness, Faust signs a pact with him. They leave on a trip through the universe. When Don Gusman and Octavio arrive in Faust's room, they find it empty.

II,1: The next morning, Don Juan and Leporello appear in the governor's garden. When Donna Anna approaches, Leporello disappears. Unaware that Don Juan is nearby, she confesses her love for him but swears she will remain true to Octavio. Don

Juan makes his presence known and tries to win her, but she rejects his advances. Hearing Don Octavio approach, he hides. From his hiding place, Juan makes comments about Octavio which reflect his contempt for social conventions. When Donna Anna and Octavio leave, Juan swears that he will kill his rival. Then he arranges with Leporello to create an incident that will allow him to challenge Octavio.

After the Spaniards have left, Faust and the Black Knight, having returned from their journey through the cosmos, appear. Faust is dissatisfied because the Devil cannot reveal to him the cause and purpose of creation. When the Knight shows him a picture of Donna Anna, however, Faust demands that he help him in winning her.

II,2: We find ourselves in a hall in the governor's house. Signor Rubio, the police director, and Signor Negro provide comic relief with their conversation. Don Juan and Leporello appear, followed soon by Faust and the Devil, who produce horror and confusion among the guests. Faust tells the Knight to prepare a castle on Montblanc for Donna Anna, whom he will kidnap. According to their own plan, Leporello creates an incident with Octavio, whom Don Juan then kills in a duel. But when Juan tries to claim Donna Anna, the object of his machinations, Faust steps in and abducts her. As soon as Faust has left, however, the Knight betrays the German magician's destination to Don Juan. To avenge Octavio's death, Don Gusman challenges Don Juan to a duel.

III,1: Don Juan kills the governor in the duel. In dying, Don Gusman pleads with his opponent to liberate Donna Anna from Faust and to put her in a convent. Don Juan answers that he cannot lie; he refuses to renounce her. (Don Juan's great effectiveness as a character stems not only from his wit but also from his own combination of honesty and deceit, honor and cynicism.) Obviously, he has lied before, particularly in Act I. Yet he is sincere when he tells the dying governor that he cannot lie about his intentions regarding Donna Anna, for Juan can lie about everything but his own character.

III,2: Faust, the Knight, and Donna Anna are on Montblanc. Faust, who is now convinced that love is the most important force in the world, pleads his love to Donna Anna, who rejects him. She mentions Faust's wife, who is Grabbe's own invention—perhaps as a contrast to Don Juan's eternal bachelorhood,

or to emphasize Faust's inherently bourgeois character as opposed to the asocial nature of Don Juan.[1] With a magic word
Faust kills his wife, to free himself. But Donna Anna is horri-
fied until he tells her that Don Juan has killed her father. She
asks Faust to avenge Don Gusman.

III,3: Don Juan and Leporello are climbing Montblanc. Faust
meets them in a wild region. After an exchange of their respec-
tive views of life—the climax of the play as far as the relationship of the dual protagonists to one another is concerned—Faust
has Don Juan and Leporello carried away in a windstorm.

IV,1: Don Juan and Leporello find themselves in a church-
yard in Rome, to which they were transported by the wind.
They are standing near the statue of the slain governor. In good
spirits, Don Juan, ignoring the possibility of arrest for the murders of Octavio and Don Gusman, commands Leporello to prepare a festive meal for that evening. Tomorrow he will set out
anew to liberate Donna Anna. He is in such good spirits that
he invites the statue of Don Gusman to his banquet. The statue
nods its acceptance.

IV,2: Faust is seen in the mines under Mountblanc conversing
with the gnomes, who ridicule him. The magician asks them
for a potion that causes so much pain that he will forget his
pangs of love; but even their drink is not strong enough: the
mere sound of Donna Anna's name is, he says, more powerful
than all potions. In Faust's efforts to combat pain with even
greater pain, we note once again how indebted this play, like
its predecessors, is to *Weltschmerz*, that is, as F. J. Schneider
asserts, to pain as the fundamental concept of existence.

IV,3: Back in Faust's magic castle on Mountblanc. In a long
monologue Faust expounds on the pain of unrequited love: that
she does not love him is death, but that she loves another is hell.
Donna Anna enters. After a lengthy exchange, in which she
repeats her hatred of Faust, he kills her. When the Knight appears, Faust exclaims: "Dead! Gone! What is the world? It·is—
it was—worth a great deal: one can love in it! And what is love
without an object? Nothing, nothing. The girl I love is everything—over the body of Donna Anna I realize that fact. Man is
poor. Nothing great, be it religion or love, comes directly to
him—he must have a lightning rod! How happy I could have
been if I had not already sold myself to Hell when I first saw
this woman." The conditions of the pact have been satisfied:

Faust now knows how he "could have found happiness." He continues: "In these tears I am weeping I sense it: there was once a God, who was demolished—we are his pieces—language and melancholy—love and religion and pain are only dreams of Him." In an hour, he says, he will surrender himself to the Devil, but first he wants to tell Don Juan of Anna's death, so that he, too, will suffer from her loss.

IV,4: The play ends in a majestic hall in Don Juan's house. The Knight appears and says that both Faust and Don Juan will soon belong to him: the former by his own volition, the latter by the hand of more pious spirits. Juan and Leporello appear and are soon visited by Rubio and Negro. Rubio wants to arrest the Don but is dissuaded by the importance of the name and rank. Juan ejects the ludicrous police director and his companions.

Faust appears and tells Juan that Donna Anna is dead. Instead of feeling desperation, as Faust had hoped, the legendary lover says that Faust has destroyed his own heaven but that he will seek new fields to conquer. Faust admits that Don Juan is right and surrenders himself to the Devil, whom he vows to combat through all eternity. The Knight strangles him.

The Knight has been invisible to Juan, who now begins his banquet. The statue of Don Gusman appears and asks Don Juan whether he will repent. Juan answers: "What I am, that I shall remain. If I am Don Juan, then I am nothing if I become another! I would much rather be Don Juan in the abysmal sulfur than a saint in the light of Paradise! You have asked me with a thundering voice, and I answer you with a thundering voice: no!" The Knight seizes him and exclaims, "You, Don Juan, I am taking with me—to join Faust! I know that you are both striving for the same goal, yet traveling on two different wagons!" They disappear in flames, and Don Juan's last words are his hypocritical motto, "King and fame, and fatherland and love," an expression of contempt for those very values. The flames spread and engulf the house and Leporello.

In a letter to Gubitz on March 7, 1828, Grabbe calls *Don Juan und Faust* the "keystone of my circle of ideas till now" (V, 317). We must agree with this designation in as far as this play represents a comprehensive and complex statement of his ideas presented in his previous dramas.

In a self-composed critique sent to Kettembeil on January

16, 1829, Grabbe expounded his intentions: "Two tragic legends are known by the names of Don Juan and Faust: the one characterizes the downfall of the overly sensuous nature in man, the other the overly transcendental nature. This material, which has something universal about it, has been treated in tragedies, tragicomedies, and operas, and even Shakespeare's Hamlet is nothing but an English Faust. Mozart's *Don Giovanni* and Goethe's *Faust* —what masterpieces! And how bold [it is] to appear again with both stories after these masters!" (V, 321). In the course of our discussion, several differences between Grabbe's drama and the works of his predecessors will become clear. The above statement already indicates, however, how Grabbe's conception of Faust differs from Goethe's and that it will, more or less, summarize the principal aspects of his previous works.

At one point in Goethe's drama, Mephistopheles calls Faust "a transcendental, sensual lover" (*ein übersinnlicher, sinnlicher Freier*), an apt designation for the man with "two souls in his breast." Grabbe has put these two souls into two breasts. In the completely sensual and the completely intellectual man he objectifies the inner conflict of Goethe's Faust. The world of *Don Juan und Faust* symbolizes the fragmented world of *Weltschmerz*, in which man's full potential is no longer realized in one individual, as in Goethe's hero. Although there are countless parallels, most of them are inherent in the legends surrounding the historical Dr. Faustus. Grabbe's conception of the medieval alchemist and sorcerer as being only half human in nature reveals that his Faust will express not merely half as much as Goethe's hero but rather an entirely different view of life and the world. The harmony that pervades *Faust* and all of Goethe's mature works is missing. In Grabbe's document of *Weltschmerz*, the realization of man's intellectualism seems no longer compatible with his love of the sensual, and vice versa. As in *Gothland*, man feels himself torn apart by his desire to find higher truths and his conviction that he can only know his own physical sensations. The profound incompatibility of these two sensations has, in Grabbe's thinking, exercised such a strong influence on man that mankind has had to evolve two separate, legendary figures as the extremes of these two poles.

Nevertheless, as the two sides of human nature Don Juan and Faust reveal that they are subject to the same laws and fate. Theirs are parallel lives. As much as they may disdain each other, they have, as the Devil says, been moving toward the same end. But it also appears symptomatic for a fragmented world that Don Juan and Faust, despite sharing the same fate in Hell, are never united in their modes of existence. Even death produces no synthesis of the intellectual and sensual sides of human nature. In Hell itself, as we are told at the end of the play, both Faust and Don Juan will continue to display the qualities which characterize their earthly existences: the former vows to fight on against the Devil, not because he will be allied with the forces of Heaven against evil but because he will not renounce his individuality; Don Juan chooses to remain Don Juan in Hell rather than repent and go to Heaven.

A much-criticized aspect of Grabbe's play is the fact that Don Juan and Faust do not meet in a meaningful conflict. While the work is, among all of Grabbe's serious works, the one most easily adapted for the stage, such a lack of direct conflict between the main characters could represent a major theatrical flaw.

One reason for the absence of a forceful confrontation lies in the fact that there is no tangible object or issue that could precipitate it. They are both pursuing Donna Anna, but her role is ultimately that of a chance encounter with both. One could, of course, assert that if Faust were ever to fall in love he would have to meet Don Juan because the latter is trying to seduce every woman in the world. Such an argument overlooks the equally important fact that the presence of both figures in Rome at that time is never explained as being absolutely necessary. Their views of what the Eternal City offers are so different that Rome does not constitute a common meeting ground. We must, therefore, attribute their encounter there to accident or fate. But it cannot be a necessary stage in their fate, if we understand their damnation as constituting it; neither Faust nor Don Juan is damned for his actions against the other. To put it differently, the realization of Faust's true goals does not hinge on his conquest of Don Juan, or vice versa, because both characters represent the two extreme modes of man's quest for personal fulfillment. It is as if their lives were being played out on entirely different levels of existence.

At the end of Act III, Faust does confront Don Juan, but this encounter only illustrates how impossible a true conflict between them is. After all, there is never any question regarding the victor. Faust has the power of magic and can have Don Juan swept away at will. Don Juan could not rescue Donna Anna by force even if he wanted to. We cannot apply the concepts of victory and defeat here as we would in a classical drama. Don Juan does not accept defeat and seek solace on a higher plane, as do Schiller's Maria Stuart and Joan of Arc. Don Juan has not been forced to change his attitude. He simply heads off in another direction, seemingly forgetting Donna Anna. This encounter between the German magician and the Spanish nobleman has little or no influence on the plot. Its primary function is, in fact, to show that a meaningful confrontation is impossible and to reveal to the audience that Faust and Don Juan have such divergent views of life that their paths can cross in life only accidentally: Don Juan asks, "Why [strive to be] superhuman if you remain a man?" to which Faust replies, "Why [be] human, if you do not strive for the superhuman?" Their exchange of views anticipates the dialogue between Danton and Robespierre in *Dantons Tod,* in which the former's fate is as good as sealed. One of Büchner's main themes in *Dantons Tod* is that men talk past one another and that there is no communication. Danton and Robespierre are lonely men, a situation implicit in the existential modes of Don Juan and Faust as well. Don Juan and Danton are powerless against Faust and Robespierre, and the main concern of the audience is not what they do to their opponents but how they differ in their modes of existence.

Since Don Juan and Faust figuratively do not even speak the same language, they cannot really argue out their differences. It is left up to the audience to compare their characters, actions, and notions. Grabbe had already used this approach in *Marius und Sulla,* where, we remember, absolutely no encounter between the protagonists took place. There, as in *Don Juan und Faust,* our interest is directed more at the contrasting themes and images than at the details of the plot.

Don Juan furnishes, in effect, a link with Grabbe's previous dramas, particularly with Sulla, Grabbe's ideal. This is not to say that Don Juan represents his ideal, thought it must be admitted that Grabbe was justly proud of this character. Like Sulla, Don Juan is cold, logical, and contemptuous of conventional values. Nowhere are the Spaniard's traits and standards more obvious than in his attitudes toward "language," which has already been a frequent theme in Grabbe's dramas, extending back to Berdoa's ridicule of "eternity" as only a word and the Devil's contempt for the world as a "mediocre comedy."

In Act I, Scene 1, Don Juan is trying to seduce Donna Anna. When she interrupts him with the announcement that Don Octavio is approaching, Don Juan says to himself, "Damned, I was in full swing. The images were streaming out of my mouth by the dozen" (I, 449). We recognize that Don Juan is far removed from the impassioned lover the young ladies in Grabbe's audience might have expected. He is more interested in his own images than in the passion he purports to feel. One could say he is an artist of love, but a cold, calculating, self-conscious one.

Regarding language as a tool, Don Juan personifies the esthetic distance of an artist. We do not need to strain our imagination to compare him with Thomas Mann's Tonio Kröger, who is a late nineteenth-century parody of the *Weltschmerzler*. Like Tonio, Don Juan shows contempt for those who think that sincerity of feeling is necessary or even permissible in literature. When Octavio approaches, Don Juan says to himself:

Octavio did not see me. He is coming with slow bourgeois strides. I shall step aside into this decorative bush and eavesdrop on the pretty phrases in which he expresses himself. One can learn from such drudges—they have feeling—that is to say, instead of having enough imagination and spirit to play with passion and to decorate life's horizon with it as a golden wreath, they let themselves be tortured by it, scream loudly about their pain and sell this ware as an independent and individual feeling. And yet—the women are so stupid—only stupidity can conquer them. Howl with the wolves, and with the women feign piety, dance and lie! (I, 449)

A key passage in understanding Don Juan, these lines reveal his contempt for bourgeois values, his disdain for sincere feelings, his cynical acquiescence in convention, as long as it serves his purpose, and his thought as an "artist" in love and language.

Furthermore, Don Juan, traditionally the representative of the Spanish baroque culture that idealized women, has little regard for them. Not even in this limited sense can Don Juan be considered an idealist or the representative of a social ideal.

In terms of his relationship to Faust, Don Juan's remarks on feeling are also crucial. The *Weltschmerz* of Gothland and Marius, as well as that of Grabbe's contemporaries like Lenau, leads to an agonized expression of inner pain, usually about their inability to attain ideal values. When the Don calls Faust a "braggart of melancholy" (I, 424), he links him with such figures as Octavio. Verbalized pain seems ridiculous to Don Juan. Nevertheless, an interesting paradox creeps into his speech: he disdains those who scream loudly about their pain as if it were their own, individual feeling—and herein lies the implication that they are ridiculous because they think that they alone suffer and that each of us, including Don Juan, can suffer as well. Don Juan is perhaps closer to the *Weltschmerzler* he ridicules than he himself realizes. Like them, Don Juan is a lonely man who feels totally isolated from all society and convention— he, however, refuses to verbalize his pain.

Don Juan's contempt for convention is symptomatic of his rejection of all systems. He asks Leporello: "Man, do you consider me a silly pedant, rooted in systems?" (I, 425). He continues: "Wherever I find beauty I appreciate it, of whatever type it may be. The servant girl loves in a different way than the mistress, and only variety gives life attraction and lets us forget how unbearable it is" (I, 425f.). Thus, Don Juan does not relish and savor life as the ultimate joy in itself. He really finds life unbearable. He must have variety for its own sake, for any thought of goals in life is meaningless: "Away with the goal— don't name it to me, even though I might even be struggling for it—cursed is the thought: any goal is death. Well be he who eternally strives. Yes, hail, hail to him who could eternally hunger" (I, 419). Like Goethe's Faust, Don Juan strives without respite and in the hope that the next moment will bring more satisfaction than the last. In Grabbe's drama, it is Don Juan, not Faust, who is the man of action, the man with insatiable drive. He disdains systems because they would explain away the thrill of individual events by making them part of a larger plan. He says to Leporello, "Friend, only where it becomes endangered does life gain a little value" (I, 482). Life is unbearable, and it seems to have value only if one is in danger of losing it. Playing with death becomes for Don Juan, as later for Büchner's Danton, the ultimate titillation.

Don Juan is still the traditional pleasure seeker, but Grabbe has given him an additional dimension. His desire for pleasure, excitement, and danger stems from a feeling that life is unbearable. The symptom of this feeling is "boredom." And Don

Juan's life consists of an incessant fight against such boredom. But why, we ask, does he find life meaningless and, therefore, boring?

In the most revealing declaration of his mode of existence, Don Juan explains to the governor why he killed Don Octavio:

To be sure, you believe that you had the right on your side, but I believe it was on mine. The right is hundredfold, and each man exercises his own. I was guided by what guides you, me, and every human being, but is called by different names. Why does the priest pray? Why does the merchant struggle? For what reason does the king fight his battles which outdo the lightning and thunder in destruction and noise? Because they all finally want to be pleased. I am always crying my motto, "King and fame, and fatherland and love," but only because it gives me pleasure to sacrifice myself for the content of these words. (I, 472)

Like many other characters of *Weltschmerz*, Don Juan renounces, in effect, all idealism. All persons, be they priest or king, are motivated not by ideals but by their desire for pleasure. Don Juan can find no proof of ideal values in reality, and consequently he turns to the known values of pain and pleasure. In a world without discernible eternal truths, however, every action seems like every other. There is no progress toward a goal that is more important than any individual action. When every act seems just like every other, and when there is no feeling that the next act will have any effect, "boredom" ensues.

In Grabbe's time, "boredom" became the standard of those who could no longer believe in idealism. It represented the alternative to such Romantic terms as "eternity," "fate," "longing," and "God," and as such it appears as a recurring theme, for example, in all of Büchner's works. Later used by Søren Kierkegaard, the Danish theologian and forerunner of Existentialism, it describes man's state, out of which, according to Kierkegaard, man can rescue himself only by the act of willing belief. This is the path that Grabbe's Faust tries but cannot continue (I, 431). Don Juan, however, chooses complete acquiesence to the physical world.

Like Büchner's Danton, like Heine and, to a certain extent, Platen, Don Juan espouses an ethic of hedonism. Epicureanism becomes a substitute for lost ideals. If life offers nothing but one moment after another, then it can be made bearable only if each moment is as full as possible with thrills and danger, with art and elegance. Don Juan's quest for pleasure stems from his desire to escape the boredom of a meaningless existence. As a result, his is a very self-conscious striving for pleasure. Unreflective pursuit of physical enjoyment and its necessary corrollary, a cowardly flight from pain, can be found in Leporello, who is the contrast to Don Juan on the latter's own level. Don Juan is an artist of pleasure, and, as we have noted in his wooing of Donna Anna, his manner of making love is more important to him than the gratification it brings. His satisfaction comes primarily from his self-fulfillment, not from carnal release. At the end of the play, he must be true to himself, even at the cost of eternal pain in Hell—proof enough that he seeks more than mere pleasure in his quest for pleasure.

As it were, Don Juan is playing a role, self-consciously creating a legend to which he must remain true, for his reputation is the only meaning his life can have in a world devoid of all superpersonal truths. His attitude toward conventional morality and social values implies a belief that the world is only a "mediocre comedy." But we must liken his own role to that of an actor who, at the same time, flaunts his audience with the fact that he, like them, is only an actor, yet tries to insure his place in their minds by the conviction of his acting. He may show contempt for life, but it is all he has, and it is, in turn, unbearable unless he endangers it constantly and ultimately renounces it for Hell. Don Juan is everything but a simple-minded pleasure seeker, insensitive clod, or lecherous rogue.

After ascertaining Don Juan's proximity to cold and logical figures like Sulla, we might expect to find in Faust a figure of contrasting qualities like those observed in Marius. So it is. Like Marius, Faust is a *Weltschmerzler* of the type Don Juan ridicules for parading their personal agony and disappointment. Like Marius, Faust seeks an ultimate truth with which he can explain his role in the world and the fate that determines it.

In his monologue in Act I, scene 1, Faust states the question whose answer he must seek in a pact with the Devil:

Have the battles, the ruin of peoples, then, had, as their purpose, only that of fairy tales invented to teach a lesson? Are world events less than world history [as a whole]? Pity us, for history has never improved mankind. Only a Don Juan is able to enjoy millions of flowers amidst the lava of destruction and not realize that there are, to be sure, many flowers, yet they are all transitory—that there is, to be sure, distraction, but no security and tranquillity to be found where the One, the eternally blooming one, does not bloom. . . . A goal, I must have a final goal! If there is a path to Heaven, then it leads through Hell, at least for me. (I, 434)

Grabbe's Faust is plagued by the question whether any single event is less than the total of all events, that is, whether there is some comprehensive system embracing all events. Such a system would signify that there is a higher principle than mere succession. Above all, it would mean that man could see beyond the events themselves. In other words, the answer to this question would release man from his captivity in the moment, from the feeling of imprisonment felt by Gothland, who says that man only reads the good into history. From the beginning, however, Faust must concede that mankind has not been improved by history, that in terms of human values there seems to be no progress in history.

Faust sees in himself the apothesis of Don Juan's acquiescence to the thrill of the moment. Indeed, he cannot even understand how the Spaniard can content himself with the ephemeral. Striving for the superhuman means for Faust that he can free himself from the restrictions imposed by the world, that he can literally step outside himself, to see himself in a larger context. In short, Faust reflects the yearning of the Romantics for spritiual freedom. He longs for the ultimate, the pure ideal that is timeless. The eternal flower he seeks is scarcely distinguishable from the "Blue Flower" that Novalis' Heinrich von Ofterdingen seeks.

We note that Faust seeks a goal. Don Juan rejects all goals and, in doing so, becomes the man of action. In his reliance on a goal, Faust becomes what Don Juan will not be, "a pedant rooted in systems." Don Juan manipulates words and images, but Faust becomes their slave. Just as Don Juan's attitude toward language reflects his view of the world, so does, as we see in the following, Faust's position regarding the relationship between man and language.

According to Grabbe's own statement, Faust should represent the exclusively intellectual side of man. As such he lives in a world of verbal abstractions. When he makes his demand of the Devil, he asks to be shown "how he could have found happiness." Not only does he reflect the pessimism of the typical *Weltschmerzler* who, like Gothland, has renounced all hope of ever being happy; he also states his desire to learn something that can have only verbal significance. Because his wish is in the subjunctive, it has no validity beyond the confines of language.

Faust soon learns, however, that all mankind is a captive of language. After returning from a flight through the cosmos, Faust expresses his dissatisfaction: "Friend, I sought the power and purpose, not the exterior." The Knight answers that Faust would not have understood them even if he had deciphered them for him "because they lie beyond language. You men can think only what you can put into words" (I, 454). At first, Faust cannot accept that "language is supposed to be greater than man" and asks: "Feeling and longing, all the unspeakable sensations that quiver through us like thunderstorms—what are they?" The Knight answers, "Just fog, fog! Whatever is unspeakable is without sense and clarity." Faust replies: "That would mean that all humanity is only gossip! And why do I feel a thirst to discover more than language can offer?" The Knight responds: "Because you artificially stimulate this thirst in yourself. Do like millions of your brothers—sleep, eat, drink and be happy."

Like his counterpart in Goethe's drama, Grabbe's Faust seeks in essence "what holds the world together in its innermost." But unlike Goethe's seeker, he renounces experience. Don Juan's quest for new experiences brings him close to Goethe's Faust, whereas Grabbe's Faust cannot satisfy himself within the limits Don Juan has imposed upon himself, namely, of individual phenomena. Yet he must ultimately accept that what he seeks is beyond man's ken because it transcends verbalization. Goethe's Faust can overleap the restrictions of language by feeling: "Name is only sound and smoke, feeling is everything." But in Grabbe's drama words are everything, for it is not they, but the feelings which are artificial. Feeling and intuition bring no clarity, and the clarity of language has meaning only within its own context. Faust must finally concede that mankind is only "gossip," a paraphrase of the Devil's words in *Scherz, Satire* that the world is a "mediocre comedy." Here as well as there, the targets of Grabbe's attack are man's reliance on systems and, simultaneously, the Romantic's belief that he can intuit truths beyond the finite world of language and systems. Grabbe once again demolishes the Romantic belief that insights into universal truths can be stimulated by language. The true and successful manipu-

lator of language is Don Juan, the antithesis of Romantic yearning for infinity.

The Devil counsels Faust to be like other men. But we must
not confuse the Devil's description of what Faust should do
with an account of what Don Juan is doing. In effect, the Devil
is telling Faust to stop thinking about the meaning of his life.
As we have seen, the force which drives Don Juan is his conscious desire to find a substitute for a life that has no higher
meaning. Paradoxically, Don Juan, who seems to reject all attempts to be a "superman," is driven by his knowledge that he
cannot be one. In turn his incessant drive makes him almost
superhuman. Don Juan, no less than Faust, can never stop thinking about the meaning, or lack of it, in life, and acceptance of
the Devils' advice would deprive him of his individuality, just
as much as it would deprive Faust of his.

We see how much alike Don Juan and Faust are, despite their
different directions. And we realize that, eventually, they must
end together. Yet we are struck by their totally different characters. Don Juan is witty, worldly, and seemingly frivolous. Faust
appears melancholy, unworldly, and abysmally self-conscious.
Don Juan suggests a character out of a comedy; Faust, one out
of a tragedy. Although Grabbe calls the drama a "tragedy," it
is obvious that the humorous episodes are more than mere
comic relief. Don Juan is motivated by no lesser problem than
Faust, and his fate is no less tragic: he must sacrifice his highest principle—pleasure—in order to save his integrity as an individual, as Don Juan. On the other hand, the comic scenes
often hit at the very foundation of the tragic, a technique that
leads to a tragicomic structure. We have encountered tragicomic
episodes and implications in almost all of the previous works.
Now, however, Grabbe uses his gradually acquired techniques
to great effect.

Although several critics have commented on the tragicomic
aspects of *Don Juan und Faust,* Karl Guthke offers the most
penetrating analysis of Grabbe's approach, which he describes
as a "mirror technique." This designation is based on the fact
that Don Juan and Faust produce reverse images of each other.
It is, indeed, easy to find almost all of the same ideas in reverse
when these two characters are held up next to each other.
Moreover, as Guthke demonstrates, both are "striving," but each
ridicules the type of striving which the other embodies. After

hearing Don Juan's comments on Faust, the audience can no longer fully accept the picture of a tortured intellect he presents. In turn, Grabbe also undercuts the seriousness with which we accept Don Juan's mockery.

As we have seen, Don Juan is simultaneously a serious character and the satirist of Faust's character. If he is to be taken seriously for the same reasons as Faust, namely, because he cannot merely "eat, sleep, drink, and be happy," then the Don's ridicule also represents self-irony. In effect, the lover is ridiculing the scholar for being unable to enjoy life, but he himself is just as self-conscious in his own pursuit of pleasure.

But Grabbe does not leave it at that. The mocker is himself mocked: Leporello's down-to-earth approach to love sharply contrasts with the artistic fantasies and posturing of Don Juan, the supposed realist and lover. Ironically, although Don Juan is the legendary lover, the only amorous conquest in the play is not his. Leporello proves himself far more successful with the chambermaid than the Don with the Donna. And the totally unpolished servant passes himself off as a count to achieve success—an indication perhaps that Juan's nobility aids him more than his artistry.

Ultimately, both Don Juan and Faust are tragic and comic alike. If that is indeed the case, then their answers to the questions relating to man's existence are correspondingly tragicomic. Neither answer seems, in itself, complete, for each can either be accepted or laughed at. Although they never completely abandon their given characters, both Don Juan and Faust experience their downfall in terms of the other's values. The former asserts an almost superhuman belief in his own individuality and goes to Hell because of this belief. Faust succumbs to human love, and as a consequence he must concede that one can live in this world.

Their common fate manifests itself in their seizure by the Devil, who, in turn, tells us how inadequate both modes of existence are. After Faust in Act II, scene 1, has heard the Devil's advice to give up all attempts to understand the ultimate truths of life, he asks: "What shadow suddenly flashed through Hell and Heaven, while you in full glory were showing them to me? When it broke through, angels, devils, God and you yourself stiffened like wax figures?" The Knight answers that he does not know, and when Faust asks why, he continues: "Yes, for only the world, the Devil, the God whom you can comprehend do you comprehend and see!" (I, 454f.). Does this light stem perhaps from the same realm in which the angel in *Scherz, Satire* is sitting and writing his "mediocre comedy"? We receive no answer. In any case, Grabbe's Devil and the God he opposes are not the ultimate forces in the cosmos. No matter how hard Faust and Don Juan try to answer the question of man's role in the universe, the answer must remain incomplete, for the Devil shows us that something exists beyond Heaven and Hell, which represent the ultimate limits of man's comprehension.

In a sense, *Don Juan und Faust* fulfills its promise to summarize the ideas in the previous dramas, particularly *Gothland* and *Scherz, Satire,* the most strongly anti-Romantic works. But we also have many indications that this work does not simply stem from a look backward. Before it was completed, Grabbe stated his intention to devote himself to historical subjects. Following *Marius und Sulla, Don Juan und Faust* might seem like a mere excursion or simply another experiment. Experiment it is, but one that reveals a continued interest in history. Too often neglected by critics, the relationship between *Don Juan und Faust* and Grabbe's historical dramas should not be underrated, mainly because it makes his sole drama of ideas seem less isolated and, therefore, helps us to see the continuity from *Marius und Sulla* to the Hohenstaufen dramas.

We have already compared Don Juan and Faust with Sulla and Marius. In terms of character, they have much in common. Moreover, Faust, like Marius, shows an almost obsessive concern for "time," and like Marius, he seeks an answer to his questions in history. To be sure, Faust's interest appears to be largely theoretical, while Marius is caught in the web of specific political events. Yet Faust, as we see him in Grabbe's version, is a far more historical character than in most other dramas about him.

First of all, Grabbe emphasizes Faust's German character. Faust's own time was less conscious of nationalism than was Grabbe's, a fact that let Faust become an almost international symbol. Even Goethe, although he leaves almost no aspect of human conduct unexplored, does not dwell on Faust's Teutonism (of course, only *Faust, I* had appeared when Grabbe wrote his drama). Yet Grabbe's Faust says himself that he would not be Faust if he were not German (I, 431). The incorporation of the nationalistic element might be regarded as a break with the historical tradition of the real Faust, who, like his contemporaries, had a more cosmopolitan view. But Grabbe does anchor Faust in the political conditions of the late Middle Ages, when Germany was divided into many small states. The parallel between the divided Germany of Faust's century and that of Grabbe's lifetime is then exploited. Faust ends a long section of his monologue in Act I, scene 2 on his fatherland: "But so be it! It [this fate] befell me as well, and I am following my stars!— Germany! Fatherland!—and not even on the battlefield could I fall fighting for you—you are Europe's heart—yes, torn apart as only a heart can be" (I, 433). Faust's inner strife stems from his being German, because all Germany is rent by division, and he only reflects his homeland. In fleeing to Rome, he says, he hopes to take up in himself all of humanity, to escape from his Teutonism. Throughout the drama, however, it is clear that he, as Heine said of himself, "always carries the soil of his homeland on his shoes." Grabbe's Faust represents both the contemporary German desire for unity and a parallel to another time when Germany was divided. As we shall see, in his Hohenstaufen dramas Grabbe will return to a time of such unity and then show the forces that undermined it.

Faust's historical position is further solidified by his supposed relationship to Martin Luther, an admittedly important aspect of the early legends about him. Emphasis on Faust's German Protestantism gives the comparison with Don Juan, the Catholic, even more symbolic significance. But Grabbe's drama is far removed from being religious allegory. The religious issue is probably best regarded as a picture of the fall from two religions, not as the conflict between them. We recall how Schiller put the sensuality associated with Catholic art and ritual to good use in *Maria Stuart* and how he contrasts it with Elizabeth's Protestantism, which seems so abstract and devoid of physical or emotional appeal. There is, to be sure, little other resemblance between Schiller's play and Grabbe's, but we can see how Don Juan stands for sensuality and Catholicism and how Faust represents the spirit of speculation and Protestantism. In other words, Grabbe's extreme cases of human nature also carry in them the exaggerated faults of the two great religions of western Europe. And as Grabbe saw in retrospect, the religious issue was yet, particularly in the seventeenth century, to bring Europe much woe.

Faust comes from the North, while Don Juan represents the South. Grabbe does little here with the implications of such a contrast. In general, of course, we note the heavy-footed plodding of Faust, the melancholy German, as opposed to the light-footedness and grace of Don Juan, who repeatedly mentions the dance. The contrast between North and South will, however, be stressed in the Hohenstaufen plays and, for that reason, should be mentioned here in a description of *Don Juan und Faust* as a prelude to them.

Some critics, like Guthke, bemoan Grabbe's inclusion of so much satire, particularly that which is directed against the police and social establishment. For figures like Rubio and Negro do not seem to fit into the over-all pattern of the play. Yet such criticism ignores the basic tendency in Grabbe's view of the world which necessarily leads him ever closer to strict realism. *Scherz, Satire* contains much supposedly irrelevant criticism of institutions and petty problems of the day, such as the poor street lighting that makes girls into prostitutes. Yet we are not disturbed by such irrelevancies because Grabbe is simply not interested in a homogeneous presentation of the world. A world presented on the stage without discrepancies would imply that such a world exists—or at least that it could be viewed that way. But from *Gothland* on, Grabbe portrays the world as a chaos.

Moreover, Grabbe's dramas represent a continued negation of eternal, ideal principles and an affirmation that man is stuck in a world of real, historical facts. Institutions belong to these concrete facts. Indeed, they will come under increasing fire: mercantilism is attacked by Heinrich the Lion in *Heinrich VI,* usury in *Aschenbrödel,* petty politicking in *Napoleon,* mercantile greed in *Hannibal,* and the corrupt courts of Roman justice in the *Hermannsschlacht.* In *Marius und Sulla,* the episodes with Scaevola might be considered irrelevant, but Scaevola was a part of the world at that time. He represented part of the corruption that could be eradicated only by a dictator. Don Juan and Faust are rebels against society, but society is more than an abstract principle with abstract systems. It is real and tangible, just like the pleasure which Don Juan pursues or like the attraction Faust feels for Donna Anna. Don Juan and Faust represent rebels in history as well as legend; and Grabbe, through characters like Rubio, Negro, and the "proper" Octavio, shows what they were, in part, rebelling against.

The most important link with the historical dramas lies quite simply in the fact that Don Juan and Faust are "supermen." One question pervades all of Grabbe's historical dramas: to what extent can a superman control history? Even as supermen, however, Don Juan and Faust are lonely actors playing out roles on the "stage" of life, actors in a tragicomedy. Is the strongest character essentially unimportant in a world that brings out certain qualities in the individual and suppresses others? In the Hohenstaufen dramas, Grabbe deals again with these very questions.

II   *The Hohenstaufen. A Cycle of Tragedies*

First Part: Kaiser Friedrich Barbarossa. Act I, scene 1: The ruins of Milan. With the support of Cardinal Ugolini, Gherardo, the consul of Milan, incites the populace to rise up against Barbarossa, the devastator of their city.

1,2: In the German camp, Landolph and Wilhelm, men at arms for Heinrich the Lion, discuss their discomfort in the foreign country, the destruction of Milan and the close relationship of Heinrich and Barbarossa.

Heinrich himself appears as the others retire, and in a long monologue he expresses his belief that fate has willed a clash between himself and Barbarossa, whose ambition has carried him too far and must now be opposed. About Friedrich he says: "Woe, I am frightened. For the opponent is my friend and the most glorious of all men. Far more beautifully than the jewels of his diadem, the power, the high-mindedness, and the grace shine around his brow. My heart beats in my breast whenever I see him, and my breast opens like a triumphal gate to receive him" (II, 17). There is, therefore, no feeling of envy motivating Heinrich, who pleads that the voice of friendship may drown out the roar of fate.

Following Heinrich's departure, Barbarossa appears with his retinue. With great pageantry he has his vassal lords mustered. Milan is not represented, and Barbarossa declares its inhabitants traitors. He has scarcely spoken the words when ambassadors from that city and Lombardy arrive, but he has them executed. From the beginning, it is clear that Heinrich and Barbarossa are not motivated by the same feelings as other men: they are fully conscious of their historical roles.

II,1: Heinrich the Lion orders his army to march homeward instead of toward Milan in support of the Emperor. The Bavarian lords who oppose his decision are executed. In *Gothland* Grabbe paraded slaughter across the stage, in part to shock his audience. In the *Hohenstaufen,* the executions, like those in *Marius und Sulla,* belong to the period, to a time in which there could be no vacillation or lack of resolution.

II,2: Heinrich the Lion arrives with his retinue at the Emperor's tent at Legnano. During their confrontation, Barbarossa cannot convince Heinrich to support his campaign, and when the Lombards, thinking that they have found an ally in Heinrich, cry their support from a distance, the two friends almost declare an open conflict, but Beatrice, Barbarossa's wife, separates them. Heinrich leaves, and the Emperor, assured of increased strength by the remaining knights, calls for the battle despite his greatly reduced strength. In this scene we have experienced the type of confrontation missing in *Marius und Sulla* and *Don Juan und Faust.* Here, however, the confrontation is possible because Heinrich and Barbarossa, as men of similar conviction, background, and spiritual nobility, have a common meeting ground lacking in the other opponents.

III,1: The Doge's palace in Venice. Pope Alexander III receives the Archbishop of Mainz, who comes to sue for peace in Barbarossa's name. Because Gherardo agrees, he accepts the peace, although with the remark that he knows it will not last long. News is brought that Saladin has conquered Jerusalem. In Barbarossa the Pope sees the man who can defeat the Saracen leader.

Accompanied by his son, Prince Heinrich, Barbarossa appears. In order to restore his good relations with the Pope, Barbarossa agrees to lead the crusade against Saladin. Still concerned about his empire, however, he makes Heinrich renounce the German girl he loves and go to Sicily, where he is to court Constance, the successor to the throne. This action undoubtedly lays the cornerstone for Heinrich's personality as we see it in the next play.

III,2: In the Hohenstaufen castle in Swabia, Barbarossa is reunited with his wife, who gave him up for lost. The scene concludes with preparations for the Reichstag in Mainz.

IV,1: Mainz can be seen in the background. The pageantry of the medieval Reichstag is the subject of this scene. Everyone of note in the empire, including the poet Heinrich von Ofterdingen, is there—except Heinrich the Lion, who has not obeyed a threefold summons. He is promptly banned, and his land rights are revoked by Barbarossa, who calls his true followers to war against him.

IV,2: In Heinrich's bivouac, the enthusiasm and loyalty of his men is portrayed. In a lengthy dialogue with his wife Mathildis, Heinrich explains that he cannot hate Barbarossa and that he is sad because he must fight his dearest friend.

V,1: The battle on the banks of the Weser between the two friends is re-created. Heinrich and Barbarossa meet, embrace, and reaffirm their friendship but also the necessity of their battle. In their duel, Heinrich is wounded, but he and his troops are allowed to retreat.

V,2: Heinrich has lost his lands. When the scene opens, he and Mathildis are standing on the Frisian coast, from where they are leaving for England. Landolph staggers in and dies. Heinrich can only say, "I was really loved very much." The scene ends with Heinrich's oath that his family will not die out and with Mathildis' promise to nurture a worthy successor.

V,3: In the Emperor's palace in Goslar, Heinrich's lands are divided. Before he leaves for the crusade, Barbarossa has Prince Heinrich, who has returned with Constance as his bride, proclaimed emperor. The play ends with a triumphal march.

Second Part: Kaiser Heinrich VI. A Tragedy in 5 Acts. Act I, scene 1: The play opens not far from Vesuvius with a view of Naples, the sea, and the islands. The Normans Tancred, Bohemund, and Guiskard talk about their past glory and position, now usurped by the Germans through Prince Heinrich's marriage to Constance, which provides an immediate link with the preceding play, particularly with Act III, scene 1. Incidentally, it strikes the viewer of Grabbe's historical plays how often they begin with a scene of reminiscence on past glories. Such beginnings imply that even the action to come is but transitory. Such an impression is here strengthened by the arrival of Count Acerra, also a Norman, with news of Barbarossa's death.

Despite his hatred of the Emperor, Tancred must admit his greatness. In answer to Tancred's lament that the Normans are only the shadows of their former selves, the count tells him that

the barons in Sicily have revolted. Under the direction of Archbishop Matthew, he says, the people have elected Tancred king.
Accepting the scepter from Count Accera, Tancred calls for the
restoration of his kingdom's glory.

After the Normans have left the stage, Captain von Schwarz-
neck appears with a group of Swabian warriors. They discuss
their pursuit of the Norman traitors, then continue on their way.
Such interpolated, realistic portraits of the common man keep
Grabbe's drama from becoming another saccharine, romanticized
picture of the Middle Ages.

I,2: We see the terrace of the royal palace near Naples. As so
often in the Hohenstaufen dramas, there is a symbolic, far-
reaching view of the background, this time on the Gulf of Naples.
Constance pleads with Heinrich to spare her people, whom he
considers mostly traitors. He refuses, and in a monologue she
says that he does not love her but thinks only of new conquest.
We recall, of course, *Barbarossa,* Act III, scene 1, and we note
that Heinrich's renunciation of love brings him closer to Sulla
and Don Juan and removes him farther from Marius, Faust, and
even Heinrich the Lion and Barbarossa, who are shown, in the
preceding play, as being very close to their wives.

The Empress Beatrice and the leaders of the Reich arrive with
Barbarossa's coffin. Hohenzollern reports on Barbarossa's conquests, his death, and the easy defeat of his army ensuing. Heinrich swears not to pursue the dreams of fame but to practice
only pragmatic politics:

I learn, learn on your body, father! You were great, yet also too
full of generosity; you were a hero, obsessed like no other, yet
instead of reigning as Germany's ruler, you only acted like a hero!
Why the crusade and its vain fame? What good is fame if one
sacrifices power to achieve it? It alone [the power] can maintain
one. What does Jerusalem mean to us? It lies far from the lands
of the Hohenstaufen.... Dead one, you strove only with noble
means toward a noble goal. What are means? Tools! I cast them
aside when the work is completed. You knew only high-mindedness
and battle—very unequal weapons against your malicious opponents.
Let me join them in using the same weapons they use: treachery,
intrigue, money and cruelty. (II, 128f.)

The Hohenstaufen, like Faust and Don Juan, are consciously
"striving," but now the contrast lies not so much in the goals as in
the means.

The Archduke of Austria comes to lodge a complaint that Richard the Lion-hearted has disgraced the Austrian banner. Then Archbishop Ophamilla arrives with news of the Norman revolt. In order to suppress the rebellion, Heinrich allies himself with Achmet and his Saracens. Heinrich is, therefore, true to his oath: he obeys only the exigencies of the moment. He feels no remorse in uniting with followers of the faith against which his father launched his last campaign. Admiral Diephold reports that Richard has been shipwrecked in Trieste. Heinrich orders him captured and imprisoned. Diephold also says that Heinrich the Lion is rumored to be headed for Friesland. After turning over the administration of Sicily to Constance and commissioning Diephold to protect his son, Heinrich sets out for Germany to meet the threat posed by the return of Heinrich the Lion. Once again, Heinrich VI shows his sense for pragmatic values, for he is more concerned with the security of his base of power in Germany than with keeping his foreign conquests.

II,1: In a tavern in Austria, Richard the Lion-hearted, mostly through his vanity, is recognized and captured. His actions are conclusive proof that he belongs to the older generation of Barbarossa and Heinrich the Lion, to which name and fame meant more than the dictates of self-preservation. II,2: The singer Blondel finds Richard imprisoned in a tower but is also captured.

II,3: The Saxons are waiting on the Frisian coast for Heinrich the Lion. The elders must tell the younger people about their former leader, whom the children cannot remember. Here and elsewhere, Grabbe seems less concerned with the fact that glory soon passes than with the inability of the people to remember it. Heinrich the Lion, now an old man, arrives and extols his homeland and Barbarossa, the symbol of the times he knew and understood better. When he asks about the happenings during his banishment, he learns that pettiness and selfishness have been the law of the land, that the old warrior spirit has largely disappeared and that the city dwellers and the mercantile class have become unbearably proud. Bardewick, the city he had protected, has even refused to join his cause. Heinrich the Lion sets out to destroy Bardewick as a lesson.

II,4: This scene reveals the complacency and self-satisfaction of Bardewick's population. It closes with the storming of the city. II,5: Heinrich the Lion stands amidst the ruins of the city, where he has a sign, *Vestigia leonis,* placed above the city gates. A herald arrives, but Heinrich refuses to comply with the Emperor's summons to judgment. Instead, he sets out for Brunswick, which he wants to see again before he dies.

III,1: We are shown the hall of the imperial diet, in the background a throne with all of the symbols of the empire. Prince Heinrich, the son of Heinrich the Lion, and Agnes von der Pfalz, a Hohenstaufen, have married out of love and are now waiting for Heinrich VI, her cousin, to tell him of their union. They withdraw while the Emperor attends to affairs of state. He repeats an attitude common to almost all of Grabbe's kings and leaders: that the scepter is a heavy burden to bear. In a conflict of interests with the Pope, he imposes the choice of a new bishop for Lüttich for purely political reasons—once again, we have a striking contrast to Barbarossa in a not dissimilar situation.

Heinrich then summons Richard the Lion-hearted. Among other things, Heinrich accuses the prisoner of having abandoned the crusade, an accusation that would never have occurred to his father. We also recall that Heinrich has already expressed his contempt for such unpragmatic undertakings as crusades, and we recognize that he is only playing the game of deceit and intrigue he has made his own. Despite initial protests that it cannot be done to an anointed ruler, Heinrich demands ransom for Richard—after all, he swore on his father's body that he would make money more important than fame and honor. Incidentally, we understand how money could become the idol of Bardewick and how greed and arrogance could replace the principles for which Heinrich the Lion fought.

News is brought that Tancred has captured Constance, but Heinrich's son is safe in the fortress Rocca d'Arce. When he hears that Bardewick has been destroyed, he wants to kill Heinrich the Lion. But Agnes intercedes and convinces him of the political sagacity of her marriage: it frees him to move against the Sicilian rebels. Heinrich recognizes her marriage and goes to meet Heinrich the Lion. Richard expresses his admiration for his captor, who says, "I do not see just one man, I see the world." How different is his position, we realize, from that of his father, for whom the individual combat with Heinrich was all-consuming and the deepest expression of his fate.

III,2: Brunswick in the palace of Heinrich the Lion, is the site of this scene. Two servants discuss the supposed appearance of the "Woman in White," the symbol of death. Heinrich the Lion enters and, in a very long monologue, muses on the marriage of Agnes and his son. But he cannot dispel his belief that there will never be complete peace between the two families. The Woman in White appears to him and prophesies his death within the hour. She tells him how ephemeral everything will be, but she cannot, dare not, answer his questions about the final judgment and Christ. Heinrich VI enters with Prince Heinrich and Agnes. They are reconciled. Characteristically, Heinrich VI ascribes the old man's vision of the Woman in White to senility. Heinrich the Lion dies telling of his vision of Barbarossa and Mathildis waiting for him.

IV,1: In Naples, Tancred and his followers pass the death sentence on Ophamilla and Count Aversa, two followers of Heinrich VI whom they have captured by trickery. Grabbe adds balance to the rather elegiac portrait of Barbarossa's era by showing that Heinrich VI is perhaps not so wrong about his own time and the type of opponents it produces. Despite protests, Tancred—himself almost a throwback to the age of Barbarossa and its ideals of chivalry and honor—frees Constance. Then he leaves to besiege Rocca d'Arce.

IV,2: We see the hunger and disease among the defenders of Rocca d'Arce, who under Diephold and Achmet nevertheless continue their resistance. An interesting interpolation is Achmet's fairy tale, which he tells in order to lift the Saracens' spirits: it bespeaks once again, another mentality than that of the Emperor. Heinrich VI arrives with relief forces, and all go out to meet him. IV,3: The battle between the imperial forces and Tancred, who is defeated. The scene closes with Heinrich's reunion with Constance and his son.

V,1: In front of the cathedral at Palermo, Heinrich, who has learned of Tancred's death, holds court over the rebellious Normans, whom he condemns to death by quartering and blinding. Christmas is approaching, and Constance asks Heinrich to imitate Christ, but he reiterates that earthly politics must be handled by trickery and deceit.

An old woman appears, who says that Heinrich will be dead within two days and that none of his plans will have been realized. He orders her to be killed. This scene offers, of course, a pointed contrast to the appearance of the Woman in White before Heinrich the Lion's death: Heinrich VI is visited by a "real" woman, for, as the Devil says in *Don Juan und Faust*, only the things you can comprehend do you comprehend and see.

V,2: A conversation between a herdsman and his helper concludes with the former's assertion that, after all the empires have fallen, the simple peasants remain. This theme frequently recurrs in Grabbe's works, and it seems to carry the same message as expressed by the fisherman's wife in *Marius und Sulla*: "We have a small existence, and when they bother about us, it only happens in order to oppress us; we can do nothing but jump aside when the great ones fall" (I, 344). There is both triumph and tragedy in the peasant's life, above which the mighty seek their fame, fortune and power.

V,3: We find ourselves high on Mount Aetna, whose symbolic significance is accentuated by the coming dawn indicative of Heinrich's plans for an even greater empire. During the hunt with falcons, Heinrich speaks of his intentions to expand his realm. But suddenly he cries out and falls dead of a stroke. His death contrasts sharply, of course, with the almost mystic experience of Heinrich the Lion. At last, Heinrich VI sees only what he can comprehend. And because he did not accomplish his earthly ends, he dies cursing his ever having been born.

Grabbe makes his most revealing remarks about his intentions in the Hohenstaufen plays when in his self-critique of *Barbarossa* he writes "if the other works of this Hohenstaufen cycle are like *Barbarossa*, then no other nation will possess such a poetic national monument as this cycle. *Barbarossa* is a serious 'fate drama' in the better meaning of the term. The relationships are given: Welfs and Waiblings are each too great for both to exist next to one another; the Emperor and the Lion are friends, yet forced by the circumstances, they must fight each other, just as the Pope Alexander, who is there in all of his historical greatness, must also move against the Emperor, not out of common animosity and pettiness—with which many a dramatist prefers to endow the church—but rather with a similar view of the circumstances" (V, 333).

Regarding the first point: Grabbe is trying to create a "national drama." His efforts in this direction go back to his essay on the "Shakespeare-Mania," in which he calls for a national, truly German drama instead of imitations of foreign models, no matter how great. Although Grabbe cites Schiller in this context as a possible model, it is obvious from his preceding plays that he is not following Schiller's lead in his own attempts.

With his first play written after completion of his essay on the "Shakespeare-Mania," Grabbe lays his foundation in the character of Faust. By calling particular attention to Faust's Teutonism and, above all, to the inseparability of Faust's problem from the Germany of his day and Grabbe's own time, he asserts, at least for the Faust material, the uncontestable claim of Germany. But Grabbe had to look around for a subject that represented an important phase in Germany's political history.

He seems to have found the appropriate subject for his national drama in the Hohenstaufen story. In his letter of May 13, 1829, to Kettembeil, he writes: "I'm glad that you like *Barbarossa* more and more. I would rather have created it than *Götz von Berlichingen* along with all of Shakespeare's historical pieces. And his Germanness [*Deutschtum*]!" (V, 329). Goethe's *Götz* had, up to this time, furnished the model for all historical dramas of German flavor, and now Grabbe believes that he has surpassed it. We can also understand his reference to Shakespeare, not only as an expression of Grabbe's usual immodesty, but also as a statement of his belief that he had finally succeeded in creating a truly national drama. In the essay on the "Shakespeare-Mania" he speaks of Shakespeare as the national poet of England, and his *Barbarossa* augurs a similar role for him in Germany.

Grabbe emphasizes Barbarossa's *Deutschtum*. We could even find justification for assuming that he was trying to create a German myth, for he implies the precedence of the Hohenstaufen material over the most famous monument of German literature, the *Nibelungenlied*. During Grabbe's time the *Song of the Nibelungs* was attributed to Heinrich von Ofterdingen, who also appears in *Barbarossa*. Ofterdingen says in Act IV, scene 1 to his Emperor: "If I had not viewed the greatness of the Hohenstaufen, I would never have succeeded in the *Nibelungen*" (II, 82). In other words, what made the German national epic great is portrayed by Grabbe in *Barbarossa*.

By introducing Ofterdingen, Grabbe comes as close to Romanticism as he ever does in his plays. Ofterdingen is the hero of Novalis' novel, in which the apprenticeship of the poet is shown. Grabbe also suggests the foundation of the poet's greatness. But he does not indulge in Romantic mythologizing. Novalis wraps his poet in a veil of mysticism, a fairy-tale atmosphere, while Grabbe anchors his poet in a factual world that is realistically presented.

No less than the obvious realism, the recurrence of problems from Grabbe's earlier works precludes an overly sentimental, Romanticized presentation, problems that themselves stem from Grabbe's inability to accept Romantic idealism. Like *Marius und Sulla*, *Barbarossa* is a tragedy of fate: like the two Romans, the Kaiser and Heinrich the Lion would not have been forced to fight one another if they had not been born in the same century. It was their good fortune to be of the same mind, to be great at a time when greatness was appreciated, and to be drawn together by their mutual respect. But these qualities of greatness, which were brought to the forefront by the times, produce, in turn, their personal tragedy. Because their conflict results so much from the historical circumstances, these circumstances must be shown in all their breadth. Grabbe tries to capture the unique atmosphere of the times in the scenes of pageantry and in other mass scenes.

Both Barbarossa and Heinrich the Lion are, like Grabbe's other characters, from Gothland on, captives of their time. The Pope, as Grabbe states in his letter, has a view of circumstances beyond that accorded to the participants of the conflict. He admonishes the Emperor: "One sees far from the heights of the Vatican: What you were striving for can become truth. Yet you preceded your time. Whoever steps out of his time, is alienated from it" (II, 68). Barbarossa responds: "I believe that even the temporal circumstances can be overcome, for it was men who created them." The Emperor's assertion reveals the cause of his disaster, for he went beyond what the times allowed.

The Pope's complementary remark to Barbarossa's assertion, "Under God's direction," must, however, be understood in context. The Vatican and its blessing represents but one of the historical circumstances, not a supernatural force. The Pope comments on the events with great insight, but there is no indication that God is really speaking through him. In the long run, Barbarossa dies in a fruitless crusade because his time has made him receptive to the pressure of the church—a pressure that plays no role in his son's fate. Barbarossa's life is determined by the political and economic forces of his time, among them the Catholic church. Although Grabbe strips the Pope of his divine authority, he does not, as he points out in his letter, view him negatively. On the contrary, the times that allow chivalric greatness produce a great church leader. The church, therefore, reveals less about the workings of a divine fate than about historical factors. As Heinrich VI says later, "Only our opposition conferred value on him [the Pope]" (II, 176).

Another set of conflicting forces, familiar, by implication, from *Don Juan und Faust*, substantiates the factual basis of the "fateful" conflict: the division between North and South. Grabbe has brought so much realism to bear, particularly in his characterization of the lower classes, in order to reveal the basic differences between the northern and southern Germans. The northern Germans, followers of Heinrich the Lion, are a stolid, serious group, the Swabians and Bavarians under Barbarossa a lighthearted, adventurous one. The .northerners are blond, the southerners dark. The former want to return home and find the latter's excursions into foreign lands suspect. Heinrich the Lion is, therefore, both the leader of his people and typical of them. On the other hand, Barbarossa, like his followers, is far more fascinated by an adventurous undertaking and by the attractions which it promises.

As similar as he is to Heinrich the Lion, Barbarossa differs from him as the Bavarians and Swabians do from the Frisians. In the persons of the great leaders, however, such differences are raised to titanic proportions. Barbarossa's adventurousness does not simply stem from the lightheartedness of the southern German character. He says in a rare moment of introspection: "It is dangerous to fathom the deepest seeds of deeds and thoughts in one's bosom. There lie abysses, deep as hell itself, in the soul, and woe to him who descends into them" (II, 67). Nicholls describes Barbarossa's insight correctly as an anticipation of Nietzsche's statement that the Greeks were superficial— out of depth (p. 159). Barbarossa plunges into action without premeditation because he dares not think about their implications.

Heinrich the Lion, on the other hand, continues Grabbe's series of meditative heroes, who, like Marius and Faust, are always searching for a meaning, for the hand of fate. Ultimately fate reveals itself to Heinrich the Lion in the form of the Woman in White. But she tells him nothing about ultimate truths. The only satisfaction he derives from her is the knowledge that there is a fate at work, something Barbarossa already assumed in his refusal to seek the deeper significance of actions.

Grabbe projected a cycle of eight plays, but when we examine the character of Heinrich VI we understand why he never wrote more than the first two. On one side, we have Barbarossa and Heinrich the Lion; on the other, Heinrich VI. The older generation represents a different, more sentimental attitude, and the younger a colder, more rational one.

Barbarossa and Heinrich the Lion seem closer to Marius and Faust than to Heinrich VI, who incorporates many of the traits we have observed in Sulla and Don Juan. Marius, Barbarossa, and Heinrich the Lion are fanatically patriotic and are fanatically adored by their followers (see, for example, I, 398). Barbarossa and Faust are very self-consciously German. Sulla, Don Juan, and Heinrich VI are cosmopolitan and international in their attitudes. Sulla and Heinrich VI suppress any desire for fame and any feelings that might deter them from their goals, any scruples about intrigue and duplicity. Both Sulla and Heinrich VI rule by logic and by terror. One of Sulla's underlings, Kaphis, says: "Sulla's personality is too strange, too different from the usual, for me to trust him. He does not feel like us, and nobody knows whether it might not occur to him to view us like spiders and flies that a boy tears apart indifferently and without compassion because he does not understand their cries of misery" (I, 350f.). A character in *Heinrich VI* could conceivably have said the same thing about his Emperor. Sulla and Heinrich VI have strikingly similar dispositions. Moreover, in his cynical manipulation of those around him, as well as in his own ability to feign whatever the occasion demands, Heinrich resembles Don Juan.

In other words, Grabbe's protagonists in *Marius und Sulla* and *Don Juan und Faust* already possessed, on the one hand, the characteristics of Barbarossa and Heinrich the Lion, and, on the other, the attributes incorporated by Heinrich VI. The plot summary of *Heinrich VI* indicates, in part, how often Grabbe picked up threads from *Barbarossa*. Indeed, an uninterrupted performance of the two plays would be quite plausible. Furthermore, more than a mere chronological development is obviously intended, for the allusions in the second play to the first consist primarily of parallels and contrasts—as if both plays were but one. Considering that the protagonist of *Heinrich VI* represents the half of the same dualism as in the previous dramas with contrasting protagonists, we must assume that Grabbe was, consciously or unconsciously, structuring his "cycle" less on the principle of a chronicle than on that of a "mirror technique." If this is, indeed, the case, he had already said what he wanted to say after portraying the other half of a basic dualism in the second play of the cycle.

Having before us another example of the "mirror technique" used in *Don Juan und Faust*, we must ask ourselves whether it also serves a tragicomic end. The answer can only be a qualified affirmation. Grabbe calls both plays "tragedies," as he did his *Don Juan und Faust*. In Barbarossa and Heinrich VI he presents the two extremes of rulers as well as of personalities. As in *Don Juan und Faust* both suffer the same fate. We have noted that Don Juan and Faust are both tragic and ludicrous in their downfall. Here we are confronted by a similar situation.

Don Juan ridicules Faust's destruction of his own heaven, as Heinrich ridicules his father's meaningless death in search of fame. (We must remember that Barbarossa drowned on his way to the Holy Land, that he therefore never truly participated in the fighting, and that even the attempts of the remaining crusaders bore little fruit.) Seen with the eyes of cold logic, as is the case with Don Juan and Heinrich VI, the otherwise "tragic" deaths of Faust and Barbarossa seem pointless and absurd. Don Juan, however, also commits the absurd act of denying his highest principle, that of pleasure, when he chooses Hell and misery. He, too, seems slightly absurd. Heinrich VI, who has schemed and planned, intrigued and plotted, killed and tortured, dies at the very moment when the way to his goal seems clear. His life has been worthless because he has discounted means for the sake of his objectives. Since "how" he acted was of no concern to him, his life is deprived of all meaning by his failure to achieve his ends. As perfectly attuned to the world of politics as Don Juan was to his own world, Heinrich VI is but another example of a futile attempt to solve the problems of existence. This interwoven structure of the Hohenstaufen dramas, therefore, aligns them with several of the earlier plays.

Yet an obvious emphasis on the change in historical attitudes also marks the succession from *Barbarossa* to *Heinrich VI*, which shows the deterioration of the world of the Middle Ages and the rise of mercantilism and individualism. A similar transition is the subject of Hebbel's *Agnes Bernauer*. But Hebbel's drama ends on the promise of a new age, of progress. Grabbe abruptly cuts the thread leading from Barbarossa through his son into the future. Whatever change has come about is given neither historical nor moral significance.

Grabbe demonstrates his remarkable ability to rearrange and condense history, to emphasize the contrasting characters of father and son, and to capture the "spirit" of the times and its transition. But this spirit reveals nothing about the ultimate purpose of the Hohenstaufens' lives. Faust asked whether there is truly "world history" or only "world events." If anything, Heinrich's death gives us a negative answer, for it stamps his life as just another "event."

III   Aschenbrödel. *A Dramatic Fairy Tale*

Act I, scene 1: The Baron of Fineterra is sitting in his castle and discussing his situation with his servant Andreas: his mortgages are due, and after the death of his first wife, who had made life miserable for him, he has remarried—with even worse results. Only Olympia, the daughter from the first marriage, represents a consolation for his home life. His wife arrives. Her complaints are interrupted by Isaak, the Baron's most persistent creditor. The baron ejects him by force. The rest of the scene, which shows the Baroness giving advice on marriage to her own daughters, Clorinde and Louison, is interrupted by Isaak, who tries to climb through the window and down the chimney. (It should be noted that, in the original version of 1829, Louison's name is Thisbe; the later name is obviously a play on Louise, the name of Grabbe's shrewish wife, whom he had left before he began the revision.)

I,2: In the palace in the first capital of the country we see the King, Mahan, the court poet, the fool, and the royal retinue. Mahan, the King's former teacher, suggests that, in order to choose a queen, he should go to his second capital, where he is almost unknown. While the fool takes his place, the King can move about unrecognized in his search for the most noble mate. Isaak enters and pleads his case in vain before the fool as king.

II,1: A room in the Baron's castle. Olympia, the Cinderella, is preparing her stepmother and her two stepsisters for the ball. They leave with the Baron, while Olympia remains behind.

II,2: On a spring meadow the fairies at play are joined by a gnome. The queen of the fairies appears to tell them about Olympia, to whom she wants to give love and the crown. II,3: In the Baron's castle, Olympia is at work. She is visited by the fairy queen, who, after giving her costly clothing, transforms a rat into her coachman and a cat into her maid.

III,1: In the palace in the second capital, the King, disguised as a castellan, observes the goings-on. The Baron sits at a table. Olympia appears with the fairy queen and her retinue. The Baron has a conversation with the coachman, whom, because he wants to eat paper, the Baron confuses with Walter Scott. Other characters converse with the Baron about literature.

The King and the fool reappear, and the Baron is joined by his wife and stepdaughters. Olympia, when asked by the fool how she liked the play, says that she found it to be poor. Everyone is shocked except the true king, who sees in her the girl he has sought. He declares his love and kisses her. In the meanwhile, her stepsisters are fawning over the fool disguised as the King. When Isaak tries to collect his debt from the Baron, the coachman grabs and eats the note.

The true king wearies of it all. Trying to reveal his real identity, he tells Olympia that she will marry the King. Olympia, thinking that he means the fool, flees with the coachman, who is, in turn, pursued by Isaak. True to tradition, Cinderella loses her shoe, and the King sets out to seek its owner.

IV, 1: We find ourselves back in the castle. The fool tries the shoe on several women. Olympia is discovered. Isaak appears in pursuit of the coachman. The King gives Isaak his money. The queen of the fairies transforms the animals back into their true shapes. And Olympia and the King seem destined to live happily ever after.

Two comparisons naturally present themselves: (1) of the first version with the second; (2) *Aschenbrödel* with *Scherz, Satire, Ironie und tiefere Bedeutung*, Grabbe's other comedy.[2]

In its original form, *Aschenbrödel* contains more and stronger literary satire. Much of this satire is carried on by the Baron, who, in the first version, bears distinct resemblance to the Schoolmaster in *Scherz, Satire*: although he has more polish than the rural scholar of the earlier work, the Baron shows a similar both-

feet-on-the-ground approach to life. Such an attitude, at least
in Grabbe's plays, can lead only to a thorough condemnation
of contemporary literature, and so it does. The Baron, obviously
in sympathy with Grabbe's own plans for dramas on major historical figures, says to the coachman: "Listen, Mr. Unknown,
if in the future you write as nonsensically as you talk today,
you won't be popular anymore. You must always serve the
public with what you served it previously and what tastes best
because it is the easiest to digest: the most miserable, pitiful
material. Also you should dare to take up the great subjects,
like Louis XI and Napoleon. You are, of course, a genius, but
still a bit too weak to pull such people down to your own level"
(II, 281).

We also note a measure of self-parody in these lines, for they
imply that even a poetic genius would necessarily have to pull
the great heroes down to his level. This means that our own
genius, Grabbe, would also have to do it. Self-parody indeed
plays a significant role in the first version: a dialogue between
the Baron and the fool on Grabbe as a poet and man covers
two of the seventy-two pages of text (II, 292f.). The coachman
also compares himself to Grabbe's Gothland or Schiller's Don
Carlos, "who were also some sort of an idealized animal or
transformed rat" (II, 296). Such self-parody aligns the first
version to *Scherz, Satire.*

In *Scherz, Satire,* we perceived a pronounced "laughter of
desperation," a tendency toward cynical contempt for mankind. The same qualities recur in the first version of *Aschenbrödel* but are deleted in the second. Nicholls, for example, gives
an excellent account of the King's disillusionment and even
speaks of a "Kleistian ring" (p. 178) in one of his speeches (II,
307f.). Obviously, there are also anticipations of Büchner's
Leonce und Lena as well, particularly in the figure of the disillusioned and bored King.

In the original, the King says:

I would like to be angry, to doubt in man and to believe that he has
acquired understanding only to debase it arrogantly for the satisfaction of his passions, to flatter, to be hypocritical and to lie with it.
The fool plays the stupid king quite well. But since he is called
the "King," he is considered the wonder of his times. If he is rough,
the ladies and gentlemen say he is roguish. If he speaks in a silly
manner, then they regard that as the subtlest irony, and if he turns

on his heel and makes the most ridiculous leaps, this is called original and the act of genius. Even his hunchback seems to every woman to be the curvature of beauty, and his bloated face is the sun. It is true: human beings are despicable. One could easily become a tyrant and treat the people like spiders and toads. Nero's deeds are really more comic than horrible. (II, 274)

This speech, as it appears after revision, can scarcely be recognized, for it has been moderated to satisfy only the absolute necessities of the plot. If the King is going to appreciate Olympia's honesty, then he must reveal his distance from the hypocrisy and superficial values of the court. This much is shown in the second version. But the original speech above reveals a misanthropic disillusionment that has no place in the revision. It betrays a proximity to the attitudes in *Scherz, Satire* and other early plays of Grabbe. Furthermore, we note the implications of tragicomedy in the King's reaction to Nero's actions; and we are, of course, reminded of Grabbe's remark on Sulla's humor, which grows with each horrible deed. In the later version of *Aschenbrödel*, the King says simply that he can understand how easy it is to become a Nero. The tragicomic has been omitted. The moderation of the later version can be interpreted as a sincere effort on Grabbe's part to find a positive solution and to show that the ideal can occasionally be realized.

Nevertheless, satire on the court and its decadence is still present, though meliorated, in the second version, completed after *Napoleon* and before *Hannibal*. In the two major historical plays, the presentation of the court, symbolic of the "system" and artificiality, has, however, tragicomic implications more in keeping with the first *Aschenbrödel*, which can, therefore, be viewed as a transition piece to the major works. The revised, more idealistic *Aschenbrödel* appears, on the other hand, to have provided a respite between the bitter portraits of the established, fruitless, corrupt, and ignorant systems depicted in *Napoleon* and *Hannibal*. Indeed, it seems to be a last, desperate attempt to reconcile ideality and reality, for Grabbe's last drama, *Die Hermannsschlacht*, offers little more consolation than *Hannibal*.

Yet, even in its final form, *Aschenbrödel* still incorporates many themes and motifs from the earlier works, particularly *Scherz, Satire*. In turn, it continues the line of development from the previous plays to *Hannibal*, as well as having many features of *Napoleon*. No harmless interlude like *Nannette und Maria*, it is, despite its latent attempt to find a way out of the Grabbian conflict between ideality and reality, typical for the author of *Gothland*.

Unlike his fairy-tale or literary predecessors, Grabbe's coachman does not lose his ratlike characteristics. His change to a human being occurs only in terms of his appearance—in a world of appearances. The coachman-rat, therefore, continues a series of characters in Grabbe's dramas. Like the Devil in *Scherz, Satire*, Berdoa, and Saturninus, the rat comments on the plight of humanity in a devastating manner, and his words are given almost equal weight by the fact that he shares their remarkable characteristics.

Berdoa seems often to be standing with one foot in this world but with the other foot in another, demonic one: for example, when in Act I, he is injured, his recovery is nothing short of miraculous and is produced by hate alone. Grabbe's Devil, although ostensibly human, is always cold and must put his hands into the fire to keep them warm; he even retains his cloven feet, which must be reshod. In *Napoleon*, Jouve closes the first scene of Act IV with the lines: "[Who knows] whether there are not black, hellish legions in the unknown depths of the earth, which are waiting and will some day break through to destroy all the decadent glitter of the surface?" (II, 399). Jouve also implies a knowledge of a demonic realm. Indeed, as we shall see, he incorporates much of the satanic himself. Grabbe's coachman-rat is related to these figures in as far as he has acquired human form yet remains a rat, eats paper, and carries out other comic actions characteristic of a rodent.

In another comedy, it might be a harmless invention when the coachman-rat proclaims: "It's miserable to be a human being—if my beloved ever saw me, I would be ashamed to death" (II, 497). But these lines in the ¿cond version were written after *Napoleon*, in which Jouve, another character whose human existence appears suspect, asks: "But what purpose have all our foolish actions, why should a miserable swarm like this crowd of people, stumbling toward deterioration, arouse the indignation of the depths of the earth or the heights of the stars?" (II, 399). The coachman-rat's comment is too characteristic of Grabbe's other grotesque, twilight characters to be considered just quaint humor.

In *Scherz, Satire* the Devil describes Hell to Rattengift. In *Aschenbrödel* the queen of the fairies tells the coachman-rat to remain what she has made him, to live and die as a pious Christian. The coachman says that he would rather live and die in excrement (an echo of Gothland?). To the queen of the fairies, who cannot believe that he would renounce paradise, he retorts:

> I don't want to go to your heaven. I want to go to the rat-heaven—to the place where there are no human beings, no cats, no traps, no dogs, particularly no terriers—to the place where I'll find my murdered father again and my twelve children, whom I just recently ate out of pure love and hope to eat again there—to the place where every noble rat, the more he has robbed, the more he will be rewarded with grain, bacon, ham, and paper—where the rat-king with seventy thousand rat-heads sits on his throne . . . and wraps his seventy thousand tails around the world and holds it in his grip with them. I can only disdain your heavens. (II, 499)

The only difference between the revised speech and the original is the omission of the coachman-rat's claim of direct relationship with the rat-king. It is clear enough that the rat-heaven pictured here suggests Dante's Hell. Nevertheless, this is a comedy, and the rat stays moderately well in proportion to his role. What he says is only a hint of the grotesque, more disquieting side of Grabbe's cynical humor in almost all of his dramas.

Although virtually all of Grabbe's dramas treat the question of fate or destiny in some manner, the theme occurs only once here, and at that it seems almost a blind motif. At the end of Act I, the King says, upon hearing from Isaak about Olympia, the daughter of the debtor Baron: "Olympia!—it seems to me as if the name were being carried across to me from my distant childhood." Isaak has, to himself, already called Olympia a "Cinderella," but the King is not alluding to the fairy-tale figure. Grabbe distinguishes here between his character and the one familiar from everyone else's childhood. Olympia, and not Cinderella, lies in the King's future. He and she are fated, not as reincarnations or as the characters of the fairy tale, but in their own right. She is the one honest person left in the kingdom; and because the King has begun to appreciate sincerity instead of the hypocrisy of his retinue, she must be the only person he could marry. The shoe seems almost an ironic twist on a love that is determined on a realistic level. Grabbe's comedy bears about the same relationship to the Cinderella story as Keller's *Romeo und Julia auf dem Dorfe* does to Shakespeare's play. It would thus be very misleading to assert, as does F. J. Schneider, that *Aschenbrödel* represents a regression back to the purely Romantic form of comedy.

Nowhere is Grabbe's increased realism more apparent than in the opening scenes of this play, in which the Baron describes and experiences an endless series of financial problems. As in *Scherz, Satire,* there are really two parallel plots: the Cinderella story with Olympia and the King, and the story of the Baron's attempt to extricate himself from financial difficulties. In terms of the play's structure, the uniting element is the coachman-rat, who gains human form through the fairy queen's intercession for Olympia. He brings the Baron's story to a happy end by eating the mortgage held by Isaak, who, in the end, however, receives his money from the King. In both Olympia's and the Baron's situations, the solution to their problems is both magical and realistic. As things turn out, the King would have sought an honest, sincere girl until he found Olympia, and naturally he would have paid her father's debts. In both cases, the magical episodes are almost unnecessary adornments.

On the other hand, Grabbe suggests a plea for the super-natural as a part of the realistic world. In the first version (II, 289), the true King discusses art at some length with Clorinde. His remarks have been pared to their essence in the second version. Clorinde says about the play the guests have seen: "Quite natural, down to the last thread. Nothing fantastic in the piece, as in Shakespeare's or Calderón's. No, just like what one has at home" (II, 506). To this, the King answers, speaking to himself, "So let yourself be whipped, and you have dramas à la Iffland in your room"; and aloud, "My ladies, is beauty not also nature, only a higher one than usual?" (II, 506). Only Olympia understands what the King means. Clorinde's brand of realism has nothing to do with Grabbe's own realism in *Marius und Sulla* or in *Napoleon*. Hers is the local color, the obsession with detail, the harmless bagatellization of life prac-ticed by Grabbe's *Biedermeier* contemporaries. Many German writers of the day who were producing such a banal realism had learned from Iffland and Walter Scott, both of whom

Grabbe attacks in *Aschenbrödel*. In *Gothland* and his historical plays, Grabbe uses his superdimensional heroes as a counter to the *Biedermeier* glorification of everyday life. Here, however, Grabbe is trying to prove, by example, that there can be a bit of beauty and humor in the real world.

The real world remains just that, and Grabbe's realistic touches distinguish his work from the fairy-tale comedies of the Romantics, in which the supernatural realm of wonder provides the main subject. With *Aschenbrödel* Grabbe comes much closer to Ferdinand Raimund, his Austrian contemporary, than to Tieck and the Romantics, both in time and intention. But such similarity remains only superficial, even though Raimund, like Grabbe, often lets his comedies drift toward the tragicomic. In Raimund's *Zauberstücke* (magic plays) the supernatural realm, despite the realism of the earthly sphere, is more credible than in Grabbe's comedy. When Grabbe offers us supernatural implications he is most convincing when speaking through figures like Berdoa and the coachman-rat, the representatives of the chaotic, grotesquely bestial, if not outright hellish world. His fairy queen represents the benign powers, supposedly as a counter to the bestial side of the world. By comparison, however, she is but little less insipid than Nannette and Maria in Grabbe's previous attempt to portray the world of sweetness and light. The fairy queen's verse provides eloquent testimony to Grabbe's continued inability to write anything approaching light, lyrical poetry.

By and large, *Aschenbrödel* is not so bad comedy that it could not be performed today. In post-World War II Germany, however, the portrait of Isaak, the Jew, would virtually prohibit such a production. That is not to say that Grabbe reveals himself as a rabid anti-semite. His characterization of the Jewish usurer might, however, touch even today on sensitive nerves. Basically, Grabbe is less concerned with Isaak's Judaism than with his usury, a fact made more patent by reference to other plays. For example, of the two completed scenes in *Kosciuszko*, one deals with a Polish-Jewish tavern. In this scene, Moses and his daughter Rachel are almost sympathetically presented. Money, not religion, is Grabbe's target. We have seen his contempt for mercantilism in *Heinrich VI*, and in *Hannibal* we shall observe with what derision he portrays the merchants and moneylenders of Carthage. When we study *Hannibal*, written after *Aschenbrödel II,* Isaak will indeed appear, in retrospect, as an almost ludicrous prelude to the avarice, greed, and self-interest that leads Carthage to its downfall and to the destruction of its greatest hero.

CHAPTER 4

The Major Plays

I F Grabbe's most important role in the history of German literature is that of an innovator, his last three plays provide
the best measure of his originality. In their themes, motifs, and
attitudes they ensue directly from the previous works, but their
technique represents at least partial fulfillment of the tendencies
latent in the earlier plays, representing Grabbe's increasing
divergence from the main line of dramatic tradition in the
nineteenth century.

I Napoleon oder die Hundert Tage. A Drama in 5 Acts

Act I, Scene 1: This scene and III, 1 have been justly called by
Wolfgang Hegele Grabbe's greatest mass scenes. They have
probably never been surpassed by any dramatist. We see masses
milling about under the arcades of the Palais Royal. Vitry and
Chassecoeur, two former imperial guards, play a significant role
in commenting on the events and recalling by contrast the glories
of Napoleon's reign.[1] They are aware of their role in history. Vitry
says: "Yes, yes, père la Violette [a nickname for Napoleon]
played for a world, and we were his croupiers." Chassecoeur
replies: "Blood and death! If we were only still that!" and Vitry
answers: "Well, quiet, just be quiet—In our beautiful France
violets, frivolity, and love bloom every year anew. Father Violet
will also return." In this manner, the themes for the scene and
the play are stated: Napoleon, war and adventure, all contrasted
with the unending rhythm of life, symbolized by the return of
spring, and with the unending monotony of an "eternal recurrence." Life's rhythm and man's boredom are interrupted only by
the repeated resurgence of the revolution, which is symbolic of
both the capriciousness and the demonic in man. How enduring
the revolution is can be heard in a speech that Spalter finds
almost Brechtian: in it an old woman extols her table as a shrine
of the revolution (II, 332).

On the other hand, as if to emphasize the carousellike repetition of history, a boy wanders about throughout the scene and sings a song about a marmot. In the grotesque carnival atmosphere, we encounter the barker of a menagerie and the huckster for a peep show on Napoleon's great victories. Glory and absurdity tint the portrait of the masses waiting consciously or unconsciously for Napoleon's return.

Against this background, emigrants appear and talk about the *ancien règime*. About these representatives of the old order, the "system," an old officer says: "They know nothing about the Revolution with its bloody years, Philipp Vitry; that is over, but they remain as, after the mountain flood has rushed past, the blade of grass remains and perhaps even considers itself stronger than the floods that have inundated it and torn the banks apart. They did not move a straw's breadth away from themselves and their proud illusion, and Louis XVIII himself dates his regime from twenty-five years ago" (II, 331). This is the other side of constancy: the system that is self-perpetuating in its ignorance of the real world. The royalty lives in a make-believe world, as if there had never been a revolution. Their world is no less artificial than the pictures in the peep show of Napoleon's victories.

I,2: We see the great gallery of the Tuileries. An almost caricatured chorus of emigrants and citizens greets the arrival of Louis XVIII. We are reminded of the behavior of the courtiers and the fool disguised as king in the first version of *Aschenbrödel.*

I,3: This scene takes place in the royal apartments of the palace. Louis' inability to cope with the growing threat of a chaotic upheaval is symbolized by his desire for a comfortable "system": "I tell you, I would far rather be searching in Hartwell for my plants and flowers and determine their order according to Linné than to sit on the throne of France" (II, 341). Nature is, for Louis, not a matter of eternal recurrence, but of artificial stability. This scene shows Louis in conference with the Duchess of Angoulême and others, who plead with him to be firm with the masses. Over and over again, their conversation returns to Napoleon and the plots to restore him to power. But Louis remains incapable of action.

I,4: Napoleon is finally seen in a conversation with Bertrand on Elba. Hearing news of his support on the Continent, he decides to return.

II: The first scenes present brief glimpses of the different strata of Paris. II,1: A gardner and his niece are working in the Jardin des Plantes. The old man, who recalls how Buffon once walked there and established his system, symbolizes the older generation. His niece, however, has become attuned to the times. She says, as Grabbe gives the flower image yet another variation: "So— 1814 and 1815, that is the difference. It's the same with the rulers as with the flowers—every year there are new ones" (II, 356). Grabbe has subordinated even short scenes like this one to a pattern of common images and themes.

II,2: Again we are under the arcades of the Palais Royal in the presence of Vitry, Chassecoeur, and others. As the scenes grow shorter, the tempo increases and our excitement in anticipation of Napoleon's return mounts.

II,3: The hall of the palace of the Duchess of Angoulême, who discusses a poem with the Countess of Choisy. Throughout these scenes we witness the effect of rumors about Napoleon's return.

II,4: We are returned to the rooms of the King. The nobles are complacent. With the exception of the Duchess of Angoulême, whom F. J. Schneider (p. 260) calls Grabbe's best female character, no one expresses concern about Napoleon's landing in Toulon. She is the only one to press for military action and to doubt the wisdom of Louis' sending Ney to meet and capture Napoleon. The Duchess says that she will return to defend Bordeaux and tells her husband to take troops to Lyons, where Napoleon was last sighted.

II,5: This scene reveals the undercurrents set in motion by Napoleon's impending return. Fouché and Carnot meet clandestinely at the Place de la Grève to discuss their plans. They reject the Bourbons but think that they can control Napoleon through a constitution. Although the play is a long one, we are constantly surprised by the economy and conciseness with which Grabbe shows all relevant factors producing Napoleon and, in turn, produced by him.

III,1: The second truly great mass scene takes place in Paris. We see the Place de la Grève filled with people. Chassecoeur and Vitry discuss the latest events with a tailor. A product of the mercantile mentality and, in his own fashion, just as blind and self-centered as the nobility, the tailor thinks only of how the revolutionary activities will ruin people's clothing and thus create work for him. The King's coach drives past in flight.

Wild rumors spread, such as the one that the aristocrats plan to blow up the city.

The people of Saint Antoine enter singing "*ça ira*," the song of the revolution. Their leader is Jouve, who kills the tailor and hangs a police captain. Jouve, an incarnation of the bloody revolution of 1789, cries after the death of the tailor, "Go there [to the National Guard] and tell its leaders to go home immediately and with bent backs, otherwise I'll chop off their heads as I learned to do in Versailles in 1789, chop them off, so fast that their heads, if they have any will be lying on the ground before they can open their mouths to scream.—Whoever is a good patriot, follow me. Hack fingers off that traitorous tailor and stick them in your mouths as cigars of the nation" (II, 381). Grabbe studied his many sources carefully before beginning this play. Jouve, whose historical, bloodthirsty counterpart had actually been executed many years before the reign of Napoleon, nevertheless belongs to the "spirit" of the times, for, in Grabbe's view, he represents a political factor that is still to be reckoned with. In his own way, even Jouve admires Napoleon, who has already sent troops to suppress him. The "head-chopper" says: "How could the Little Corporal arrange all that so quickly? He is really a more capable fellow than Mirabeau, Robespierre or I. It's just too bad that he is a tyrant" (II, 383). Jouve, whose followers have been suppressed for a while, cynically decides to put on "polite" clothing again—as long as Napoleon is "fashionable." But he is still convinced that the "Jacobin caps" of the bloody revolution will outlast any order (II, 384). All move toward the Tuileries.

III,2: Queen Hortense, Napoleon's stepdaughter, arrives at the Tuileries and is cheered. We are struck by the symmetry of Grabbe's composition: I,1 contrasts with III,1; I,2 with this scene; and the following scene with I,3.

III,3: In the Tuileries that evening, Napoleon is seen with his officers in an attempt to restore order. We learn of the preparations of the other countries to march against France. Although Napoleon tells Hortense that he wants peace, his egotism and contempt for all of his opponents except Blücher belie his sincerity. Fouché and Carnot ask him to sign a constitution. In leaving, Fouché whispers to Carnot: "The old manner, as if there had never been an Elba" (II, 393). We are, of course, reminded of the old officer's description, in Act I, scene 1, of the nobles, who act as if there had never been a revolution.

IV,1: This scene shows Napoleon's public acceptance of the constitution, but the dialogue is between a "lady" and Jouve, who cynically comments on the goings-on.

IV,2: Back in his rooms in the Tuileries, Napoleon takes leave of Hortense and prepares to move against the English and Prussian armies.

IV,3: The stables are the setting for this scene, showing the preparations of Napoleon's horse Soliman for the march. Such brief episodes are, as is here apparent, more than mere attempts at creating epic breadth. We recognize that success in battle rests on the coordination of a myriad of small details. Moreover, after the retarding effect of Act IV, scene 1, the short episodes are picking up speed again, and the excitement about the coming battle increases.

Although Napoleon, as a "modern" leader, owes his position to his ability to coordinate large armies, the care he shows for his horse also gives him the aura of bygone days of knighthood. The first groom takes the horse to be a symbol of Napoleon's personal qualities: "Even if he is the most stubborn, unbending of all horses, he is, at the same time, the wildest and fastest, almost like——" (II, 403). Napoleon's personality is recognizable down to the lowest echelon and in the most trivial duty; no less so, and in no less contradictory manner, than that of Marius, Barbarossa, or Heinrich the Lion.

IV,4: The Prussian camp at Ligny. Blücher and Gneisenau converse about the coming battle, as do their troops. IV,5: Another scene set in the Prussian camp.

IV,6: In the French camp at Ligny, the loyalty and devotion of Napoleon's army is shown again with reference to Vitry and Chassecoeur, as well as others. The battle begins, and we see Napoleon giving commands. After ordering Cambronne and the Old Guard into battle, Napoleon sends word of victory to Paris without waiting for the outcome.

V,1: We suddenly find ourselves at a ball given for the English officers in a hotel in Brussels. We recognize the initial complacency of Wellington and his men, who are, however, shocked into action by the news that Napoleon is marching toward them. The feeling cannot be suppressed that, paradoxically, Napoleon brings out the best, not only in his own troops but also in his enemies. There follows the pageantry of the English preparations, including the march of the Scots. Here, as in the scenes set in the Prussian camp in Act IV, Grabbe impresses us with the great diversity of the allied armies united only through their fear of Napoleon.

V,2: The Prussian army is in retreat after its defeat at Ligny. Again Grabbe portrays conversations and reactions on the part of the troops, as well as on that of their leaders. Then Bülow arrives with fresh troops.

V,3-7: The last five scenes re-create the Battle of Waterloo in great detail and with corresponding masses of troops, seen as groups and as individuals on both sides. Grabbe's detailed re-creation of the battle has often been criticized. After so many cinematic spectacles we are, of course, accustomed to battle scenes presented for their own sake. One detail frequently singled out, not only for critical censure but also for ridicule, occurs in the sixth scene: Loban cries, "Fire," and Bülow answers, "Likewise." Critical condescension toward the former auditor's awkward "mistake" is, however, unjustified. Grabbe's sources, among them Walter Scott's history of Napoleon, record that the armies were within *speaking* distance of each other. Thus Grabbe's use of "likewise" is intended to communicate the surprising proximity of the forces which allows for their simultaneous appearance on the stage. Although Grabbe was, according to his own remarks, not writing for the contemporary stage, he was definitely guided by the possibilities of the theater.

The seventh scene concludes with Napoleon's admission of defeat, followed by Blücher's and Wellington's mutual congratulations. But even in defeat Napoleon manifests his familiar combination of grandeur, arrogance, and fatalism. He proclaims:

There go the enemy troops, plunging onward, shouting their triumph and imagining that they have expelled tyranny, achieved eternal peace by conquest, and restored the golden age. The poor fellows. Instead of one great tyrant, as they like to call me, they will soon have a thousand small ones—instead of giving them eternal peace, one will try to lull them into eternal apathy—instead of the golden age, a very earthly, fragile one will come, full of half-measures, foolish deceit and trifles. One will, to be sure, hear nothing more about mighty deeds in battle and about heroes, but all the more about diplomatic assemblies, formal visits of high figures, about comedians, violinists and operatic whores—until the world spirit arises, shakes the locks of the dam, behind which the waves of the Revolution and my empire lurk, and breaks them open so that the gap is filled that remained after my exit. (II, 457f.)

And even Blücher does not show unlimited optimism about the future, for he warns his men: "If the future is worthy of you, then hail! If it is not, console yourselves with the thought that your sacrifice earned a better one" (II, 459).

Napoleon is Grabbe's first serious play couched completely in prose. It is also his most immediate drama, for in it he shows his ability to make history relive its course on the stage. His task in the mass scenes might seem to have been somewhat easier because he is portraying almost contemporary events with people who, in the main, could still have been living. It is, indeed, difficult to imagine how simple people spoke during the times of Marius and Sulla, Barbarossa and Henry VI. No such temporal discrepancy exists when Grabbe re-creates the events that occurred fifteen years earlier. Yet these characters are more than documents of stenographic accuracy. Theirs is a natural, spoken language of the people, but also one of great dramatic effect.

In stating his intention to write *Napoleon* in prose instead of verse, Grabbe mentions his model: the prose of the Lutheran Bible translation, which was the result of "looking the people in the mouth," and a masterpiece of simplicity and directness that later served Brecht as a model. The characters in *Napoleon* express themselves without the stiffness of conventional stage characters, yet they manifest a terseness, succinctness, and wit that gives the scenes dramatic impact and concentration. This original stage language represents one of Grabbe's great accomplishments, and it will also characterize the speech patterns in *Hannibal* and the *Hermannsschlacht*. Indeed, many of the linguistic innovations attributed to Büchner and to Hauptmann can already be found in Grabbe's major historical dramas.

It might well be moot to ask whether Grabbe ever showed the dramatic concentration necessary to produce a long, serious play. But there can be little doubt that in *Napoleon* he earns the designation as one of the masters of the stage. Almost every scene is, in itself, a small masterpiece. Such is the underlying assumption of all attempts to evaluate Grabbe's skill as a dramatist. Some critics, like Hegele, demonstrate rather convincingly that there are, in fact, connecting links between the

scenes and acts. But even Hegele must concede that the cohesion of the first four acts is lost in the Battle of Waterloo,
mainly because such characters as Vitry and Chassecoeur, who
link so many earlier scenes, do not reappear.

Perhaps Grabbe believed that Napoleon himself would provide the unifying force, and that his presence, or the implication
of it, would furnish the necessary cohesion in much the same
way, let us say, that Schiller's Wallenstein unites the three plays
about him. For example, although Wallenstein does not appear in
Wallensteins Lager, everything said and done in the prologue
is directed toward his appearance in the second part of the trilogy.
But there is no such intention in Grabbe's drama—at least it is
not so obvious. And even if Grabbe had, like Schiller, limited
himself to the absolutely pertinent, if he had channeled all of
the action as carefully as Schiller, his efforts would have
stranded on the personality of Napoleon himself, whose role, as
Friedrich Sieburg points out, is a monologic one.

Like Elizabeth, Maria Stuart, and Schiller's other historical
characters, Wallenstein has the recognizable personality that
allows for personal tragedy in the classical manner. As Max
Spalter has indicated, however, Grabbe's Napoleon is too many
things to too many people, including the audience. Spalter concedes that only such a man could have played the role which
Napoleon played in history; and only such a man can, in Grabbe's
play, stay master of the many factions and forces portrayed.
Schiller's characters are set off against history; but Grabbe's
are in its midst. Quite simply stated, the more we see of Napoleon,
the less we understand him. The more we know about him, the
less able we are to judge him. The more other characters say
about him, the more we comprehend his historical position, but
the less we can fix him among individual types. Our problems,
however, only reflect the problem which Grabbe himself
encountered.

In all of his previous works, Grabbe makes it clear that he likes
the hero to be strong, glorious, and powerful. Such heroes
create a mystique about them. Barbarossa is like a figure, Grabbe
implies, out of the *Nibelungenlied.* The lives of his heroes seem
to be the glorious chapters in an otherwise meaningless history
of the world.

In his review of the correspondence between Schiller and
Goethe, Grabbe incidentally speaks of Napoleon in a tone that

implies a similar heroicizing of the Emperor: "With Napoleon's end, the world seemed to be a book read to the end, and as if we stood, as cast-outs, before it and repeated and thought about what had happened" (IV, 93). As we see in the play, Napoleon does, indeed, intoxicate the world; he does spur both friend and enemy to great achievement. He is, in fact, a man with so many talents that we can only see his abilities but not his person. Napoleon's last words were confirmed in Grabbe's own time, a banal, empty, artificial time, which the Devil describes as a "mediocre comedy," that is, as Napoleon says, replete with "comedians, violinists and operatic whores." Napoleon falls, but his life and age restore adventure and excitement to man's existence. During the battle, Napoleon says to his wounded soldiers who are being carried past him, "You poor fellows don't know either why you are sighing and groaning—forty years from now, the street songs will state the reasons" (II, 450). Their common adventure will furnish the material for the street ballads, for the book that Grabbe describes above as being ended with Napoleon's defeat yet still being read.

Yet while no one can doubt the heroic proportions of Napoleon's and the world's, last glorious adventure—and that is what the "Hundred Days" in the title symbolize—Grabbe does not merely glorify Napoleon. His play is far removed from the hero-worship or *Führer* complex for which Grabbe is often unjustly praised or criticized. In his letter of July 14, 1830, to Kettembeil, Grabbe writes about Napoleon: "He is a fellow who was driven by his egotism to use his time. Besides selfish purposes he, as a Corsican, that is, half-French, never knew what he was striving for. He is smaller than the Revolution, and basically he is only the tiny flag on its mast. . . . Not he, but his story [*Geschichte*] is great. His spirit is good and capable; he was often victorious . . . but by what means was he victorious? He never had a great opponent: his opponents were promoted by seniority, he by spirit . . . for that reason the Revolution, where something could emerge from the mud [*Kot*], resembles him" (V, 346).

Vainglorious, selfish, yet with a good and capable spirit, Napoleon realizes that he owes his former triumphs to the revolution and to fate. At the end of Act I, he bases his decision, in part, on the hope that these two forces will, once again, carry him to victory. Turning toward the sea he exclaims:

Amphitrite, mighty, blue-eyed maiden—you have already let me
court you in vain—I should flatter you, and I would rather, as a
man with weapons, wrest you from the hands of the merchants
who want to measure you, a goddess, with a yardstick and want to
make you their slave—but I know you still love him, that son of
the Revolution. Once you forgot your frivolity and carried him
with steadfast arms from the pyramids to the little bell tower of
Fréjus—tomorrow you will carry me from Elba once again back
there. Amphitrite, slumber sweetly. (II, 354)

Napoleon remembers all too well his defeats at sea by the
English, "that nation of shopkeepers," as he is reputed to have
said. But fate has also been kind to him, and even the goddess
of the sea has aided him.

On the one hand, Napoleon's knowledge that he has not
achieved his triumphs on his own merits alone gives him an
insight into his historical role. It means for him, and for us, the
audience, that he will have to share the stage with the revolution,
which bore him, and with fate—in whatever form she chooses to
appear. On the other hand, this knowledge, although it explains
in his or our eyes why he became so great, does not diminish his
stature. Indeed, Napoleon's obsession with fate—as Alfred Bergmann shows, a characteristic trait of the real Napoleon—gives
him a role in modern times that is almost comparable to that of
Barbarossa, the protagonist of a "fate drama in the better meaning of the term."

In his portrayal of Napoleon, Grabbe thus illuminates his own
problem in understanding the historical figure by suspending
his dramatic re-creation between several sets of contrasting views.
Napoleon is selfish and vain yet recognizes that he is, simultaneously, the instrument of greater powers. He is both the
manipulator of history and its puppet. Because he is so talented,
he must be taken seriously as an individual, yet as the "tiny flag
on the mast of the Revolution," he can seem ludicrous in his
posturing. Moreover, we, like Napoleon, realize that his "story"
is, in part, the product of tangible, historical factors, in part,
however, another question about the meaning and existence of
higher powers. Like Grabbe himself, Napoleon is contemptuous
of the petty, mercantile forces of modern life that demythologize
human existence, yet his own life furnishes the most telling
testimony for the impotence of human greatness in such a world.

The revolution shares the stage with the Emperor, its greatest son. The mentality and the brutality that created the ruins out of which Napoleon arose still smolders in Jouve. And since the revolution is, by nature, opposed to any existing order, it represents one of the forces that simultaneously buoy Napoleon up and threaten to inundate him like the Bourbons. As we see it through Jouve, the revolution is more than a political, historically isolated event; it erupts periodically but always from the same source—the demonic, chaotic, irrational, destructive urge inherent in the masses. As the catalyst for this eruption, Jouve has almost satanic overtones. As if sent from the depths of Hell, where time has no meaning, he will outlive Napoleon, and the "Jacobin caps will, after all, outlast everything" (II, 384). As Nicholls points out, Jouve is the adversary whom Napoleon must conquer and suppress if he wishes to stay in power. And nowhere, we see, is the combination of fact and fate in Napoleon's life more obvious than in the half-mythical, half-real figure of the "head-chopper." Although Napoleon's troops suppress Jouve's forces with surprising ease in Act III, scene 1, we sense the ever present threat of his demonic powers. They represent the stormy sea carrying the new ship, the new order whose flag is Napoleon.

As Jouve himself concedes, Napoleon is the greatest of the Revolutionary heroes, greater than Mirabeau or Robespierre. He is a superb coordinator and general—even though his opponents were not history's greatest tacticians. In the play, however, Napoleon's greatness is undercut by his personal weakness, particularly his vanity and self-deception. Yet Grabbe does not level criticism from the standpoint of middle-class morality, like the *Biedermeier* poets who glorify the natural modesty becoming a mediocre person.

There is no more bitter, disillusioned voice in all of Grabbe's works than that of the amoral, satanic Jouve, who says in Act IV, scene I that Napoleon looks majestic "as long as he knows that the crowd is watching him. At home he is, according to circumstances, moody, cheerful, garrulous, like everyone else. When he goes out, then, if in doubt, he first consults with the comedian Talma about his facial expression and how to drape his robes. (*to himself*) It's all really only a comedy. Soon it will be hard to distinguish between the theatrical princesses and the real ones" (II, 398). History as a "mediocre comedy" and the vain Emperor as a mere Grabbean actor in it—how typically cast a situation. Jouve closes the scene with a question addressed to himself:

"Yet why should our silly actions . . . arouse the wrath of the depths of the earth or the infinity of the stars?" (II, 399). Napoleon is an actor, a comedian, not because there is a divine, more glorious power beyond, but because man is insignificant. Man's actions do not seem important enough in the universe for one to take them seriously.

Seen from Jouve's perspective, Napoleon's obsession with "fate" can be considered as ludicrous as his posturing on the balcony. For example, Napoleon says: "Not peoples or warriors have forced me. It was fate" (II, 350). How far he might be going in his self-deception can be recognized in his conversation with Hortense, where he claims that he wants peace but circumstances force him into war. Yet we are reminded of Heinrich the Lion, who also wants peace but must fight. Perhaps Napoleon's emphasis on his personal fate is but another way of expressing the same idea as Jouve, namely that he is only a puppet. After his defeat at Waterloo, Napoleon observes: "General, my fortune falls, not I." What he thinks is unimportant. What matters is his fall from power. Napoleon's fate has nothing to do with the working of divine retribution in classical drama. He seems to be only a puppet with no more metaphysical significance than anyone else.

Nevertheless, in this world, which, as so many of Grabbe's characters say, is all we have, there is grandeur even in his role as a figurehead. Hortense admonishes Napoleon to flee to North America, but he answers: "My dear, a citizen who once rebelled against his monarch can go there, but Napoleon cannot flee or hide himself. If he is not destroyed or guarded like fire, Europe pursues him with rage or love. North America, by the way, will, within forty years, become a greater Carthage, the Atlantic Ocean a larger Mediterranean around which the Old and New Worlds encamp. How long, dear Hortense, will that, however, last? Two or three pitiful centuries, and then the rulers of man will wander on the islands and coasts of the still boundless Pacific" (II, 400). With the same view for greater contexts as Jouve, Napoleon realizes that the present events are but a moment in history.

Napoleon mentions Carthage, a recurring symbol for past greatness in Grabbe's dramas. In other worlds. there will be new ages of greatness like the former ones, and each will be lived out to the fullest. The Emperor recognizes that even he is no longer his own master. As a "son of the Revolution" he cannot claim that he has achieved greatness without the helping hand of circumstances. Once given his role in history, however, his personal greatness makes him no less a slave of history, for through his ability he creates a "role" for himself that he must play out. When we see the fanatical loyalty of his followers and the determination he awakens in his foes, we realize how true his evaluation of the situation was. As a "tiny flag," Napoleon represents the most important symbol of the revolution and the era it spawned. Like the flowers, like the past and future leaders of nations, and like all of Grabbe's heroes, Napoleon will disappear. But he will leave a grand legacy of adventure, for he will have played a role in a story that is more important than he. Grabbe's image of Napoleon's life as a play emphasizes, to be sure, the tragicomedy of man's ephemeral glory. Yet it also implies another perspective from which we can view Napoleon's story: it is exciting and "itself dramatic" (V, 339), regardless of the personality of the main actor or its relevance to ultimate reality.

In the dramatic conflict of Napoleon's life, there is a second force, too often ignored by the critics: the system. Like the revolution, the system knows no temporal limitations. It is a permanent element in man's life, no less so than the chaotic and destructive part of his nature. Napoleon becomes temporary master not only of the revolution but also of the system. He brings the order and coordination of the diverse elements that Jouve could never have achieved. Yet in his arrogance and personal vanity, he is comparable to the very regime that was destroyed by the revolution. Like the Bourbons, he forgets nothing, nor does he learn anything, or so it would seem from the comment by Fouché at the conclusion of Act III. He is great only by comparison with what Grabbe sees in his own time. As Napoleon says after his defeat at Waterloo, peace will come, but it will be a spiritual apathy of the same type as that which he destroyed. Such an order and the system that perpetuates it are aptly described by the conquered "son of the Revolution" in terms of a "mediocre comedy." Even if his appearance on the stage of history is, indeed, as Jouve claims, only that of an actor, and even if he himself merely created a new version of the "system," at least his life was so exciting that forty years later men will still sing about it. The world of Grabbe's dramas offers little more consolation.

None of Grabbe's other protagonists are presented as objectively as is Napoleon. He is not a sentimental idealist like Barbarossa and Heinrich the Lion. Nor does he represent Grabbe's early longing to become a human machine suppressing all emotions and gaining an undeceived and undeceiving view of circumstances like Sulla, Don Juan, and Henry VI. Nor, despite his awareness of fate and its unjust incomprehensibility, does Napoleon give in to the same *Weltschmerz* outbursts as do Gothland, Marius, and Faust. More than any other hero in Grabbe's works, he appears to be the product of specific historical forces, and like history itself, he is too complex a phenomenon to be explained with reference to conventional values.

Yet, as a product of Grabbe's pen, he also manifests some of the traits already observed in other figures. The Duchess of Angoulême, in answer to a suggestion to have Napoleon tried by jury, says: "[Turn] him [over] to the jury? People, don't you know who his jury is? The armies of Europe and no other. O weapons, weapons, weapons! ... Landed. Pity my poor heart. Now he is making his tigerlike leaps, as once he did from Egypt to Paris, from Eylau to Madrid, from Madrid to Vienna, and to Moscow. Oh, I already feel his claws" (II, 365f.). Like Don Juan and most of Grabbe's other protagonists, Napoleon is beyond good and evil, at least beyond normal concepts of guilt and punishment. Moreover, he is like a tiger. Throughout the play, Grabbe uses plant images to express order, be it the natural one of the annual flowers that come and go like rulers, or be it to show the sterile one of Louis and the previous Bourbons indulging in botany. In this garden of natural and artificial orders, Napoleon is the tiger, an animal completely beyond the rules of the flora. Gothland compares himself frequently to a tiger, and Faust loves like a "tiger" (I, 476, 494). The role of animal images in Grabbe's works has been investigated by, among others, Nieten and Weiß. Here, we are concerned only with the fact that Napoleon is both subject to the great, meaningless cycle of nature and history, yet at the same time outside of it, as are many of Grabbe's other "supermen."

Here, in Grabbe's most "realistic" drama up to that time, we nevertheless sense the typically Grabbean tone, a "laughter of desperation." Napoleon is a special case in history—he received a "second chance." By limiting himself to the period of this second chance—the "Hundred Days"—Grabbe shows not only what made Napoleon great the first time, namely the revolution, but also what gave him his second opportunity. There exists a need for him, for a time of excitement, for a stimulus to greatness. There is permanence in what he represents, for his concluding speech, despite its arrogant boastfulness, contains more than a grain of truth. There is a world spirit that will rise again, although it has nothing in common with the Hegelian *Zeitgeist*. Nor does it resemble the progressive spirit of Hebbel's historical dramas.

Napoleon's life represents another element in an "eternal return" (Nietzsche's "Wiederkehr des Gleichen," later seen). He is the symbol of an ever recurring force. But he is unique, in that he, through returning, seems to have escaped the irretrievable past and to have overcome the undulations of history. Napoleon seems to be Fortuna's favorite. But like Henry VI, he has been singled out and raised up only to be cast down again. And we are forced to ask ourselves whether there might not be some malicious humor lurking behind the events.

In a letter to Otto August Rühle von Lilienstern written on August 31, 1806, Heinrich von Kleist writes: "It cannot be an evil spirit that stands at the summit of the world; it is only an uncomprehended one! Don't we, too, smile when the children cry?" Kleist, however, asserts, almost by force of will, the benign quality of God, who smiles about our fate because he has greater wisdom. Throughout his life, Grabbe denied this quality. In Napoleon's fate, there might be a force laughing while we cry. In his drama, our only recourse seems to be not the Kleistian leap to a favorable conclusion but the laughter that Jouve applies— laughter not from wisdom but from despair. Jouve, not Napoleon, is Grabbe's spokesman for such *Weltschmerz* views, but of necessity: those around Napoleon do not regret his fate as much as their own, be it as Grabbe's contemporaries faced with a period of intellectual stupor, or as men who realize how little man can know about his lot. And like Jouve, we can only realize, in seeing the "comedy" of Napoleon's life, how insignificant our own existence is.

II Hannibal. A *Tragedy*

Act I: "Hannibal ante portas", scene 1: Carthage. Brasidas, a young man, tells Alitta that he loves her. She, an orphan who has found a new mother in Carthage, encourages Brasidas to join

Hannibal's army in Italy. It is interesting to note here how Grabbe, without mentioning Dido's name, subtly alludes to Carthage's founding by a woman—and it will be the women who finally contribute to Carthage's last moment of greatness and thus strengthen our feeling that the wheel has come full circle.

1,2: The great marketplace in Carthage. In another of his effective mass scenes, Grabbe shows the commerce of the most powerful trading city of ancient times. But the people's indifference to the war is revealed when they show themselves more interested in the arrival of a camel train with new goods than in Hannibal's victory at Cannae. An effective contrast to the previous scene is produced by the bargaining over slaves, particularly eunuchs and slave girls: love and patriotism, both sincerely felt by Alitta and Brasidas, have become mere chattel for the rest of the Carthaginians.

1,3: In Hanno's palace in Carthage, Hanno, Melkir, and Gisgon, elected by a secret ballot, whose result is not made known, represent the supreme triumvirate in the city. Their cunning and duplicity reveals itself in both personal and political matters: jealous not only of the wealth of the Barkas family but also of Hannibal's success at Cannae, they plot betrayal.

I,4: The Capital in Rome. Hannibal is besieging the city. The Romans decide to send an expedition under the Scipios to attack Numantia in Spain and thereby to cut off Hannibal's supplies.

I,5: Before Rome. For the first time, we see Hannibal himself. From the Carthaginian council's letter, Hannibal recognizes that he can expect no more help from the mother city. He, therefore, decides to withdraw with his seventeen thousand men, collected from all nations, to Capua. Hannibal is the complete realist. He tells the messenger from Carthage to touch his grandfather's feet with the hand that has shook Hannibal's. When the messenger offers to kiss the grandfather's feet, Hannibal answers: "No, they easily become dirty" (III, 101). Sentimental attachments to friends and family, disillusioned sobriety and bitter humor mark Hannibal's character throughout. Ominously, he asks Turnu, a Negro chieftain, for a bottle of poison to carry with him. As dramas, Grabbe's *Napoleon* and Büchner's *Dantons Tod* have often been compared, yet as a character, it is not Napoleon but Hannibal who stands closer to Danton. After observing the attitudes and values of the Carthaginian masses, we realize that Hannibal, like Danton, has been reduced to a "relique."

II: "Numantia and Capua," 1: The still glowing ruins of Numantia greet us. Throughout the scene, the poet Terence comments on the events. The Scipios accept the allegiance of the people there, who have been living as conquered subjects of the Carthaginians. The Romans decide to attack Carthage itself.

II,2: In Capua Hannibal discusses with Brasidas the unfit replacements sent by Carthage. Then he receives word that Hasdrubal, his brother, has defied the triumvirate in Carthage and is now moving to join him. In this episode we recognize the completion of the break between Hannibal and the Moloch worship of the Carthaginians. Hannibal says at first: "Thank you gods, for I can, for once, pray to you. Terrible Moloch, I often believed that we roasted infants in vain for you. You inhaled the delicate smoke with your distinguished nose, as if it were merely a customary tribute. No, finally you want to save Carthage—till now you have only tested it. I was mistaken about you. Hasdrubal and I! The Capitol is destroyed as soon as we unite" (III, 109). When Hannibal is told, however, that his brother is marching over the Alps, he almost loses consciousness. He refuses to see a physician, for he has a "little apothecary with him." He continues, "Moloch, I lied. I was, indeed, mistaken about you! Why did you not give Hasdrubal even the slightest warning? He [wants to go] across the Alps with that small army? Brasidas, doesn't he know that they destroyed half of my army in order to feed their vultures?" (III, 110). Although Hannibal does not as violently give vent to his frustration and anger with whatever powers may be guiding his fate, his situation is that of a *Weltschmerzler:* he has always doubted the existence of higher powers, and he can attest to their existence only when they seem to want to destroy him. Knowing no alternative, Hannibal prepares to march out to meet and assist Hasdrubal, even though Fabius has the city surrounded with a numerically superior army.

II,3: A street in Capua. After Hannibal's departure the people celebrate their freedom, but the fat, former despot, whom Hannibal has deposed, enters with his slaves and puts a quick end to their rejoicing. Everything is back where it was before Hannibal's arrival. We recall the conditions in France while Napoleon was on Elba, and his prophecy of what would happen after Waterloo. Here again we have a reminder of the pointless cycle of history, and how each year brings new flowers and rulers.

III: "Farewell to Italy," 1: A valley near Casilinum. Hannibal's scouts have confused Casilinum with Casinum, his intended goal. Hannibal, as strict an administrator of justice as Sulla and Henry VI, has them crucified. Finding himself encircled and seemingly trapped by Fabius, Hannibal prepares oxen to look like troops and then has their tails set afire to make them charge into the Roman army.

III,2: Fabius mistakes the animals for frenzied soldiers and retreats.

III,3: On a broad, beautiful plain at Cajeta in autumn, Hannibal watches the vintagers and their comic satyr play after the harvest. We note the recurrence of the "play" as a device to show here, as in other dramas, the discrepancy between this world and another, perhaps more meaningful one. Furthermore, here in the bucolic game is another example of the idyllic, that functions as a rupture in the crushing flow of events. As Benno von Wiese in his *Deutsche Tragödie von Lessing bis Hebbel* points out with regard to several of Grabbe's plays, we realize in the idyllic the limits of the historical phenomenon. But the play motif takes a bitter turn when a Roman in disguise slips up and drops Hasdrubal's head in Hannibal's lap. All those around him cry, "How terrible," but Hannibal remarks soberly, "Good, the play ends the way it must—with a stage trick" (III, 118). Themselves a prophecy of Hannibal's fate, these words manifest his growing contempt for historical greatness and his increasing awareness of the nihilism of man's existence—the main theme of the play motif. Hannibal orders the march back to Capua.

III,4: Upon hearing of Hannibal's return, the slaves in the castle of the despot in Capua revolt. When they learn that Hannibal is leaving for Carthage, they join his army.

III,5: On a hill near Capua, Hannibal bids a sorrowful farewell to Italy and takes a handful of grass with him. This is one of the rare moments where Hannibal reveals his innermost thoughts. He waxes almost sentimental: "Let my misfortune of many years excuse, even to myself, a moment of sentimentality" (III, 121). Perhaps fate's cruelest trick was that Hannibal was not born a Roman and did not defend and fight for a people worthy of him. All that Hannibal has to show for seventeen years—and ultimately for his life itself—is a handful of grass. (Shortly after completing *Hannibal*, Grabbe communicated to Schreiner a few fragments from a contemplated drama on Alexander the Great, among them: Alexander: *dying* "Bury me in a kingly fashion!" A Persian: "Depend on us." Alexander: "Yet hang my right hand out of the coffin, white, naked, as it is. It held the entire world, and nothing remains for it" (I, 342). Had it been completed, Grabbe's *Alexander* would probably have had much in common with *Hannibal*.)

III,6: The fleet at anchor. Messengers arrive from Carthage and tell Hannibal that he is to return to defend the city. III,7: On the deck of Hannibal's departing ship. Turnu has tested the men by trickery, but, even though they are mostly mercenaries, they are now completely faithful to Hannibal.

IV: "Gisgon," 1: In his palace in Carthage, Melkir meets with Gisgon and Hanno, whom he offers poisoned wine, but they do not drink it. They then conspire and order Hannibal to stay outside the walls of the city and fight the Romans there. Through their window they see, however, that his fleet is moving into the city. Melkir escapes and leaves the other two to their fate, but they, too, manage to flee.

IV,2: In the marketplace in Carthage, a herald from Hannibal calls for volunteers and puts a price on the heads of the council members.

IV,3: In the palace of the Barkas, Brasidas and Hannibal talk to Alitta. Even before she meets Hannibal, who left Carthage before she was born, she says: "Great deeds, like his, are rooted deeper than under the forehead, where they only develop. Truly, I feel that, in a small way in my own bosom" (III, 129). Like Barbarossa, Hannibal seems to be superficial out of necessity, for, once again, Grabbe implies that the hero could not be heroic if he looked beneath the surface of man's existence. Hannibal, despite the fact that the Romans outnumber his mercenaries four or five to one, resolves to meet them in battle.

IV,4: The Roman camp near Zama. The strict discipline demanded by the Scipios is shown, and the religion of Carthage is discussed; once again the cruelty of the Moloch worship and the burning of children is emphasized.

IV,5: On the plain between the two armies, Hannibal tries to bargain with Scipio the Younger. He offers him all of Carthage's provinces but refuses to submit to "Roman mercy." Scipio says that, had Hannibal been in his position, he would not have acted otherwise. In this scene, we again perceive echoes of a "fate drama in the better meaning of the term." Hannibal sounds the charge and the battle begins.

IV,6: From the tower over the main gate to Carthage, the gatekeeper describes the battle to a boy. Hannibal is defeated and forced to flee. The contrast to the recreation of Napoleon's battle at Waterloo strikes us. Not only does Grabbe make more concessions to the demands of the stage; here he also emphasizes that Hannibal has lost the battle before it begins and that there is little tension in its development and outcome. Napoleon has a "second chance" not accorded to Hannibal.

IV,7: Carthage. In front of the statue of Moloch with hands glowing from the many sacrifices, the children are still being taken from the mothers to be sacrificed. Melkir, meaning Gisgon, calls for a more important sacrifice, but Gisgon incites the mob to take Melkir, the eldest instead. Although the doom of Carthage is virtually assured, its leaders still contend for personal power. A Roman messenger negotiates with Gisgon and seems to be satisfied with the territory, money and ships offered.

IV,8: After the above demands have been met, however, a second Roman appears and demands the destruction of Carthage and its rebuilding elsewhere under another name. Symbolic for his recovery of lost values and of former feelings of honor and glory is Gisgon's refusal to give up the name of "Carthage." He calls for a renewed and final defense of the city. Ironically, Carthage will, at least, go down in the glory of battle, a fate to be denied Hannibal, whom the city has betrayed. It is, however, just retribution that the Romans' duplicity has sealed the fate of Carthage: after making the first retributions to the conquering Romans, Carthage was too weak to have any chance of successful defense.

V: "King Prusias," 1: In Prusias' palace in Bithynia. An episode with one of his subjects shows the ludicrous vanity of the King: he thinks that the subject's sneeze ridicules his name (*prusten* = to sneeze violently). Hannibal enters and asks for asylum, which is granted. But he must listen to Prusias' lecture on generalship.

V,2: Back in the Barkas' palace, Old Barkas, the grandfather, and Alitta see that the city has been totally destroyed. After sending Turnu with word of Carthage's final defense and defeat to Hannibal, she puts a torch to the palace.

V,3: In Prusias' palace, a praetor from Rome demands that

Prusias surrender Hannibal. Under the threat of war, the King gives the order to turn the refugee over to the Romans. Then he goes hunting.

V,4: In a villa near the capital. Turnu arrives and tells Hannibal of the destruction of Carthage. Hannibal, suspecting that Prusias is going to surrender him to the Romans, takes poison with Turnu. Prusias returns with Flamininus, the praetor, and his retinue.

Prusias: Here you will find him.

Flamininus *sees Hannibal's and Turnu's bodies*: Yes, dead.

Prusias: Dead?—Can you ask for more?

Flamininus: Yes, we wanted him living in front of the triumphal chariot.

Prusias: If I had not been hunting, you might have found him alive.

Flamininus: You should have refrained from hunting. I'll report everything in Rome, and the Senate will decide how you are to be punished. *Exit.*

Prusias: What—? But there is time, and something will occur to me. *With very restrained and ceremonious voice*: Now the moment in life where I must do what I have prophetically written in many a tragedy has arrived: to be noble and kingly toward the dead! (*He takes off his red coat.*) Hannibal was, as I have often said, a rash, thoughtless man—the hospitality that I showed him cost me quite a bit of effort—but he was, after all, my guest, and for that reason let his faults, and his ancestry be forgotten: I shall cover him and them with this royal cloak! As Alexander did with Darius!

His entourage (*wants to shout its approval*): O—

Prusias: Wait—this fold on the corner of the cloak does not lie right—let it not be beneath me even to correct that.

His entourage: Hail Prusias, the greatest of Kings. (III, 153f.)

Grabbe, according to his own statement, modeled Prusias after Friedrich von Uechtritz, a mediocre poet and dramatist whom he had known in Berlin and later. But the concluding scenes are not intended as literary satire. Neither Uechtritz' play *Alexander and Darius*, nor Uechtritz personally, or even the mediocre literary contemporaries as a whole are being attacked. Bithynia is another Byzantium, and Prusias' court represents all the decadence symbolized in history by the Byzantine Empire.

In the twentieth century, William Butler Yeats still sees in Byzantium the realm of pure forms. For Grabbe, writing almost a century earlier, the love of form and unity, of permanence and beauty, has already deteriorated into blind adoration of the "system" for its own sake.

During Prusias' lecture to Hannibal on the direction of warfare, the following conversation ensues:

> Prusias: That is the way man is: he sees the most remote, nebulous star before he sees his own mistakes. Then, my friend, there is no system in your battles. Sometimes you have your cavalry right, sometimes left, again in the middle, and with your infantry it is the same way.
>
> Hannibal: Let my apology be that I had to take advantage of the opportunities offered to me by the time and place.
>
> Prusias: That does not count, neither in art nor in war. Only the system is eternal, and according to this principle all armies must behave, all poems must be ordered. And the System does not die, even though it may be fallible. (III, 146)

Prusias appears ludicrous, and one could well conceive of him as a figure in a comedy. Yet there are darker overtones. Prusias suggests to us such figures as the Captain in Büchner's *Woyzeck* or Saint Just in *Danton's Death*, both victims and tyrants of a "system." Cruelty and inhumanity always lurk behind blind acceptance of systems for their own sake, for the "system" is autonomous and without concern for the individuality of each man.

As Benno von Wiese points out, the court of Prusias is a world of "automatons." Soulless men perpetuate soulless forms and rituals. Wolfgang Kayser, in *The Grotesque in Art and Literature,* shows that puppets, automatons, marionettes, or rigid bodies and faces frozen into masks and disguises are a continuing source of the grotesque. Grabbe has already used such grotesque effects as the mingling of human and animal traits in *Napoleon*, Act I, scene 1, and in *Aschenbrödel*. The murders in *Scherz, Satire* are pure grotesque. And throughout his works Grabbe suggests that history is a meaningless cycle, a pilotless carousel. But nowhere does he use grotesque distortion and caricature with such telling effects as in the Prusias scenes, in which the systems of the scientists in *Scherz, Satire*, the botanical systems of Louis XVIII, and the social and metaphysical systems opposed by Don Juan are solidified and deified as *the* system. Kayser calls the grotesque a confrontation with insanity. Hannibal, the rationalist whose activities are dictated by the requirements of time and space, is confronted by a world in which time and space are no longer relevant. Man has become completely enslaved by his soulless forms and rituals.

In one of his letters, Grabbe writes that Hannibal appears in history like a "cold myth." By the time he created the present play, Grabbe had become too sophisticated to give Hannibal "life" by making him sentimental. As has been noted, Hannibal occasionally lapses into a more tender or elegiac mood, but by and large he remains the cold realist reminiscent of Sulla, whose bitter humor he shares. To make his protagonist less "cold" and more "human" Grabbe holds him up against an even colder myth, the myth of the autonomous system. Like the actor of a tragedy who appears on the stage on the wrong evening, Hannibal suddenly finds himself in the middle of a "mediocre comedy." All at once we feel compassion for him, not only as the character in a tragedy, but also as an actor who knows that he is only an actor. And ultimately we feel remorse about the genre of tragedy itself, for it is not allowed to run its full course. The tragic must accede to the comic and the farcical. Hannibal's role in the play of life is tragic, but his personal fate dissipates itself in an absurd comedy of empty forms. Hannibal and the role of the tragic hero in general thus becomes ludicrous and unreal.

Grabbe prepares us well for the conclusion. The scene with Hasdrubal's head introduced as a climax to the peasant play foreshadows Hannibal's own death with a "stage trick." In Act II, scene 1, Scipio the Elder says to Terence: "What is tragic is also amusing, and vice versa. For I have often laughed in tragedies and almost been moved in comedies" (III, 104). Nevertheless, we are unprepared for the bitterness of the grotesque ending, an ending that, as Kayser says about the grotesque in general, deprives us of all orientation. The last scenes represent a parody of Hannibal's life, but also of the play itself. Grabbe implies that Hannibal should have died as heroically as did Alexander or Darius, but he did not. As in *Scherz, Satire*, we are left with a "laughter of desperation."

Grabbe is also concerned with the "idea" in history, in this case the reason for Carthage's downfall. In order to show the correlation between Hannibal's fate and Carthage's, he allows himself more freedom with historical fact than in any of his other dramas: he has condensed the events of both the Second Punic War (218-201 B.C.) and the Third Punic War (149-146 B.C.)

into Hannibal's lifetime (247-183 or 182 B.C.). He changes
and manipulates Hannibal's Roman adversaries to suit the dramatic unity, and he even omits Hannibal's tenure in the government of Carthage after his defeat at Zama in 202 B.C. This
omission is particularly significant in as far as Hannibal introduced financial reforms that led to a new flowering of the
defeated Carthaginian economy. Hannibal was, however, ultimately forced to flee, and after varying fortunes as a general
serving under several kings, he met the end portrayed in the
play. But Grabbe does not distort the essence of Carthage's
story as much as one might assume: after Hannibal's defeat,
his mother city never regained its full military power, and when
the Romans offered their terms, including the destruction of the
city, in the Third Punic War, the Carthaginians at first accepted,
then rejected them. Carthage was completely razed by the victorious Romans in 146 B.C., approximately thirty-six years after
Hannibal's death. In letting Hannibal outlive the city, however,
Grabbe demonstrates his historical perspective, for in fact Hannibal's fame has outlived Carthage's, and without Hannibal,
Carthage would probably have occupied no greater niche in
history than any other of Rome's countless opponents.

Moreover, the issues are presented in Grabbe's drama much
as they appear in history: Hannibal was defeated primarily by
the national unity and determination of the Romans. The feeling
we still have for the permanence and organization of the Roman
Empire permits us to accept Grabbe's manipulation of the Roman
generals. No single opponent defeats Hannibal, the greatest
general of the time, but he is crushed by a machine of conquest.
One can almost, as in the case of Hebbel's Agnes Bernauer, say
that the "wheel of history" has passed over him. But unlike
Hebbel, Grabbe does not concern himself with the direction of
this wheel: the play does not close with what new vistas have
been opened up for Rome; indeed, it does not even close with
a sense of liberation from a threat, as in the case of Napoleon.
The defeated French emperor prophesies unheroic times to
follow. From the character of Rome we may assume a similar
fate for the ancient world after Hannibal.

It might seem strange that Grabbe, after his success with a
contemporary subject like Napoleon and the still present forces
of decadence and revolution in Europe, would turn to the historically unique case of Hannibal. Yet there is a contemporary

context. As Nieten shows, *Hannibal* found acceptance among the Young Germans, the social reformers of Grabbe's day. The play's appeal to liberally oriented reformers can be recognized in the accents Grabbe sets.

Although Carthage has always been known for its commercial success as a trading city and for its institutions of slavery and human sacrifice, Grabbe emphasizes its mercantile greed beyond the needs of historical accuracy. Max Spalter goes so far as to say that Grabbe's *Hannibal* "is the closest thing to *Mother Courage* in the drama of the nineteenth century" (p. 189). Duplicity and avarice on the scale of the Carthaginians in *Hannibal* seem, especially after the satire in *Scherz, Satire, Napoleon,* and *Aschenbrödel,* to have contemporary significance. In such times—not unlike his own, Grabbe implies—the great hero would necessarily go unsupported and unappreciated.

In a letter, written about this time Grabbe states that the most objective is often the most subjective. Hannibal simultaneously symbolizes Grabbe's own plight and that of modern man in general: isolation. Hannibal as the "isolated man" makes this play not only the most personal but also the most "modern" among Grabbe's major works.

Even more so than Napoleon, Hannibal leads an isolated life. For example, his followers are the "orphans" of the world: Alitta, the mercenaries, and the freed slaves. Like Henry VI and Sulla, Hannibal has a diverse army drawn from many sources, but unlike both of them, he instills an incredible loyalty in his followers. Henry and Sulla control by discipline, as does Hannibal, but theirs produces terror and not loyalty. The silent, lonely, and strict, but not unfeeling leader of the Carthaginians naturally becomes a rallying point for the peoples who have no other loyalties, no other roots in a brutal, lonely world. Like Büchner's Danton, Hannibal attracts the offal because he is himself an outcast of society.

We cannot avoid inferring that Grabbe felt himself equally isolated, for the restraint and the almost telegraphic brevity of the language implies a conscious suppression of too strongly felt emotions. The language of this drama is a masterful exercise in understatement. It is language without flow and beauty. In describing the syntactical peculiarities of the style in *Hannibal,* Walter Weiß rejects the categories of nominal or verbal style in favor of a reduction to particles, which replace verbs (p.

240). He concludes that this style reflects a primitiveness before the categorization of language into forms of "being" and "becoming." It is this quality which, according to Weiß, makes the language of *Hannibal* more successful than the primitive speech of Galomir in Grillparzer's *Weh dem, der lügt*. At the same time, however, we realize that the language of *Hannibal* approaches pure expression, not as description of one's feelings, but as a series of ejections, as a forced reply to a world that does not allow any beautification or explanation. Pared to its essence, Grabbe's dialogue here is a direct precursor of Expressionism and Absurdism.

III   Die Hermannsschlacht

The play consists of a "Prelude," "First Day and Night," "Second Day and Night," "Third Day and Night," and "Conclusion." In other words, although there are five clearly defined divisions, Grabbe has consciously avoided the designation of "acts" in favor of a structure dependent on the content and time of   the events.

Prelude (*Eingang*): In the Teutoburg Forest, on a mountain between Aliso and Detmold, the merciless discipline of a Roman detachment on its way to Varus is experienced when a veteran of many campaigns is executed for disobedience. The Romans capture a Cheruscan, whom they force to lead them; but when their path is blocked, he escapes.

2: In Hermann's home, Thusnelda is shown as a housewife. Varus, the Roman commander, joins the household for dinner but is revolted by their food. Far from glorifying the everyday life of the Germanic tribes, Grabbe shows their customs, both appealing and unpleasant, in great detail. Richard Kuehnemund considers Grabbe's intentions to be satirical: the picture of the Germans here is far from heroic and, indeed, justifies the Romans' contempt toward them (pp. 99-102). We must remember, of course, that Varus is an unwelcome guest, and it seems highly probable that the Germans wanted to spoil his appetite. After Varus leaves, Thusnelda regrets her hypocritical friendship with the Romans and resolves that, if Hermann accepts further indignities from them, she herself will lead the opposition.

3: Near Detmold (Grabbe footnotes the name with its

etymology as a *Volksgerichtsstätte* [people's court]). A praetor
and his scribe hold court over such Cheruscans. The discrepancy
between the formalized system of Roman law and the Germans'
feeling for justice can be recognized. Hermann seems to acqui-
esce in the patently corrupt "system" of the Romans.

4: Hermann's home. In answer to his wife's complaints about
his friendship with the Romans, Hermann confides his true plan
to her: while he leads the Romans to the Harz Mountains, with
whose inhabitants he wants to meet secretly, Thusnelda is to
collect the tribes and destroy the Roman roads. Indeed, throughout the play the Germans are little more than conspirators.

5: At the foot of the Grotenburg, Varus inspects and com-
mends his veterans. When Varus asks a soldier why he does not
see a physician about an open wound on his left temple, the
veteran replies: "May it remain fresh and open rather than that
the physicians repair and do their fumbling hokus-pokus on me.
I received it one morning when the divine Julius paused at the
Rubicon and meditated, and we had to wait under the arrows of
Pompeii's troops for his decision." Varus responds with a salute,
"All honor your scar. It is one of the commas of world history"
(III, 335). After asking another soldier, Varus continues: "It is
an endless business to ask for more. Almost all of these icy-white
heads carry in scars the record of their triumphs. And these
heroes with bones of ore and hair of silver I am supposed to
use against that Nordic rabble and its loathsome climate?" We
recognize that the long series of victories has led to a cold,
impersonal, often corrupt machine of Roman law and justice.
Yet these veterans attest to the nobility of the Roman tradition,
and although Varus may occasionally seem cultivated to the
point of decadence, his feeling for tradition and culture, and for
the record of history, stems ultimately from a background alien
to the Germanic tribes.

Hermann arrives to lead the troops. The differences between
him and the cultured Roman are shown. Hermann, although
educated in Rome, says to himself: "Humanity? A Latin and
conqueror really does have beautiful expressions for tyranny.
Civilization? That sounds a bit more like it, for I want to civilize
you and make you part of our country, secure, safe—three feet
deep in the earth and with a hill of eight foot above you. Or
even better, [to give] your flesh to the ravens, and your bones
to the rain, so that they will be bleached like the best yarn" (III,

336). A few seconds later, he looks about and pays tribute to "Germany's" meadows, mountains, valleys, and men. It is for them that he wishes to fight, for he sees Rome as an invader that has come to defile and exploit them. We know Varus and the tradition to be something noble, yet we now understand Hermann's patriotism. Strengthening the appeal of the Germanic leader, Grabbe has Varus say to him, a few lines later: "You have studied your Horatius Flaccus badly, or you would not use such a common simile" (III, 337). This statement, made at such at time, could have come from someone like Prusias in *Hannibal*.

6: Thusnelda's love for her son, Thumelico, and her disagreement with her father are the subjects of this scene in Hermann's home. Her father remains friendly with the Romans and dislikes Hermann because of a supposed insult.

7: In the Harz Mountains, one of the Chatti visits Hermann, and they conspire. Varus appears later and tells Hermann that the weather has changed his plans and that he wants to return to Cherusca.

First Day: Morning. The Romans are on the march. Hermann reveals his true intentions and joins his people. The battle begins. From the start, however, it is clear that Hermann is fighting for an entirely different goal than his people can comprehend. Hermann shouts, "Germany!" One of his soldiers comments: "He speaks often of that. Where is that place 'Germany' anyway?" But no one in his army knows what "Germany" means, and least of all do they feel united under that name. Hermann can only answer: "Just let us strike now and always together and the different names won't do any harm. (*to himself*): I must attain my goals with more modest but more immediate means" (III, 353). From here on, it is apparent that only Hermann, the German educated in Rome, can grasp such a concept as "Germany." Paradoxically, he owes his vision to Romans like Varus, who have taught him to think in a historical manner and to grasp a context greater than tribal tradition. Thusnelda arrives with supplies and twenty thousand men. The battle sways back and forth.

First Night: 1: Varus converses with Eggius, the eighty-year-old commander of the nineteenth legion. He speaks of Syria, where he was commander for sixteen years until relieved by Pontius Pilate. We sense Grabbe's irony: regardless of what happens, Varus was destined to take part in one of the great events that ushered in the end of the Roman Empire: the defeat of the Romans in Germany or the birth of Christ. More than a slight implication of "fate" governs not only Hermann but also his opponent, yet we shall never learn what power or principle is involved. Suddenly, Hermann jumps over the Roman wall and steals the eagle of the nineteenth legion. Varus orders the execution of the carrier and the guard of the eagle.

2: The simple soldiers in the German camp are portrayed. Once again Grabbe reveals his almost naturalistic grasp of local color and the manners of the peasants. Otto Nieten has correctly observed that the historical times are given less emphasis, however, than the place of the battle. Hermann concludes the scene with a monologue in which he considers the necessity of total victory, and once again he speaks of a common fate for all of "Germany."

Second Day: The battle rages. In desperation Eggius falls on his sword. Varus, contemptuous of the old veteran's supposed desertion of his responsibilities, has his body stripped of its armor. Yet a few lines later, Varus himself admits that he may have to follow Eggius' example.

Even at this perilous moment, however, Varus is disturbed by a scribe who needs some papers signed. We learn what is so important that it must be signed in the heat of battle: "The document concerns the transfer of several estates located here which you [Varus] presented to Quintus Acerba and which he sold to Marcus Manius several days ago. The latter party, who has already made a payment of twenty thousand sesterces for the lands, requests me, in the case of circumstances under which the land could easily be lost to the Cheruscans, to send him a copy of the bill of sale so that he, if he loses his possession, can undertake in Rome some means of regress against the enemy, who, it seems to me, is *in dolo*" (III, 364). We are reminded of the Carthaginians, for whom the hero of *Hannibal* fought. The avarice and decadence of the Romans threatens the existence of the tradition for which Varus is fighting, and we cannot suppress the feeling that in his case, as in Hannibal's, the reason for the ultimate fall of his homeland is reflected in its treatment of one of its most loyal generals.

The pressure against the Roman position increases.

Second Night: 1: Varus senses that the battle is lost and mulls over the previous refusal of Rome to heed his advice: "We won't get through! If Eggius still lived, I would have someone to whom I could unburden my pain. As long as the wheel of the world revolves on its axles, people will say that the cowardice and stupidity of Varus lost Augustus his best legions.—And I say that my post was too far advanced, and I often wrote to Rome about it but was not heard. They imagine that Germany's forests can be controlled by police as easily as the parallel streets of Italian cities. Oh, they do not know the bushes and the vermin underneath them" (III, 366). He tries to discuss his situation with the scribe, the only other educated man in the camp, but the latter appears a mere automaton of the law and does not realize the importance of current events.

2: With the leader of the Chatti, Hermann discusses the unity of the Germanic tribes after the battle, but he receives no support for his plans. While the Romans lack Varus' realistic view of the situation, the Germans cannot comprehend Hermann's imaginative one.

Third Day: Hermann prepares for another attack. When his slaves revolt, Segest, Thusnelda's father, flees to Varus. Despite his affirmation of continued loyalty to Rome, Segest is executed, for, as Varus says, a traitor to his own people will soon become one to foreigners.

Third Night: Varus inspires his troops to one final attack. They are defeated. Even in his last moments, Varus is plagued by the scribe with more documents. Varus' words just before he ends his life once again point up a parallel to Hannibal: "I did what I could. I am better than the reputation that posterity will bestow on me. I was betrayed—doesn't that often happen to the best man first?" (III, 375).

Hermann arrives and demands Varus' surrender. He promises the conquered Roman good treatment, to which Varus answers: "I prefer to take care of myself." He then falls on his sword. Hermann says: "Even in death a phrasemaker. Let us leave him here for our vultures and ravens." We question, however, how much of a "phrasemaker" Varus was. He spoke one, unemotional sentence, but Herman seems enraptured with his own rhetoric when he continues to speak to his allies: "Give me your hands. They are dead, the oppressors. Our freedom, however, rises up like a giant above these mountains and looks with the intoxicated view of joy far toward future times and our grandchildren.

People will not forget us and this day as long as the German language is spoken" (III, 375).

Hermann's followers immediately crucify the scribe and other representatives of Roman "justice." Then Hermann tries to convince them that they should press on toward Rome itself, but they only want to return home. Hermann leaves the stage with the comment: if the Romans could only know how nearsighted the Germans are, they would be little concerned about Varus' defeat. Richard Kuehnemund calls the end "burlesque banality." This judgment would relate this play to *Hannibal* but it seems somewhat overstated.

Conclusion: Rome. Augustus is dying. There is a suggestion that his wife has poisoned him, that his son Tiberius will, however, be a tyrant and frustrate her plans. Augustus prophesies a rebellion of the patricians against his successor. He sees himself as a good actor now departing the stage. News is brought to him of Varus' defeat. He predicts a storm from the North and the advent of a new time from the East as well, for he has already heard rumors about Christ's birth. Augustus advises Tiberius, however, against taking countermeasures. The conclusion reveals that Varus' struggle was but a vain effort to stem the unavoidable deterioration of the empire.

There is little discrepancy in the critical opinions about *Die Hermannsschlacht*: it is generally considered to be the weakest of Grabbe's later works. Most critics emphasize its essentially "undramatic" character. The flaws are usually ascribed to Grabbe's declining health, for one of the most obvious weaknesses lies in the author's inability to infuse into this play the same dramatic force, unity of purpose, and sharpness of characterization found in *Napoleon* and *Hannibal*. It seems almost as if Grabbe himself no longer had had the strength to give.

For example, the minor characters in the preceding two dramas—indeed, in all of Grabbe's historical plays—are in the main drawn with the deftness, sharpness, and economy of an artist. The sure hand which, with a few strokes, portrayed Saturninus in *Marius und Sulla,* Jouve, Vitry, Chasseceour, the Berlin Jew in *Napoleon,* Brasidas, Turnu, and Alitta in *Hannibal* —that hand seems to have lost its precision and to betray the physical deterioration of the man. Schneider and Nicholls, among others, point out that only three characters—Hermann, Thusnelda, and Varus—are really rounded. The mass scenes, elsewhere Grabbe's forte, are, in *Die Hermannsschlacht*, almost banal enough to give them, as Kuehnemund contends, the effect of satire. The realism of these scenes cannot be underestimated, yet they lack the inner vitality, the dynamic force of the earlier ones. As Hegele skillfully demonstrates, they are, moreover, not as successfully integrated into the play as a whole.

Moreover, the prefiguration of the material, which has been treated by Klopstock, Kleist, and countless minor poets, contrasts sharply with Grabbe's previous subjects and with his personality. Although Faust and Napoleon, in fact even Hannibal, appear often enough in other dramatists' works, they are not as readily associated with the propagandistic implications of the Arminius story. Arminius is, as Schneider points out, an almost impossible subject, mainly because we know so little about him and his times. As a result, he, more than Hannibal, seems like a "cold myth," a myth that functions mainly as a national symbol. Grabbe sensed the personal banality of Kosciuszko, and for that reason refused to complete his play about the Polish national hero. Swayed by his own brand of patriotism, however, he seemed less objective in his evaluation of a German national symbol. Schneider compares Grabbe at length with Kleist, but he also concedes a fact that, in effect, undermines any comparison: Kleist was writing propaganda, while Grabbe was not. We recognize that the questioning, skeptical, and cynical mind behind *Napoleon* and *Hannibal* was ill-suited, by nature and talent, to treat a subject that, because we cannot overlook its patriotic significance, virtually demands a tendentious purpose. Ultimately, however, the conflict of Grabbe's disillusioned view of the world and life with the almost necessarily positive view of Arminius as a national hero makes an evaluation of his play both difficult and revealing.

The Arminius play by Grabbe is not a success, neither in terms of its prefigured material nor as a drama. But to deny it any redeeming qualities attributable to Grabbe's own talent and personality would be unfair. Rejecting the *Hermannsschlacht* merely as a product of a degenerating mind and body is grossly unfair, for, although Grabbe no longer had the physical qualities necessary for the execution of his ideas, he did have ideas, new ideas, that stem directly from his previous works. To be sure, he was following a long tradition of works on Arminius, but he pursued a line that obviated either unbridled patriotism or its antithesis, satire of a national myth. Either view presupposes a one-sidedness which Grabbe—despite his many other failings —never evidenced.

Quite simply stated, Grabbe tries to reveal the problematic nature of culture in a historical sense. In most of his later dramas, the main problem concerns some historical form of the conflict between the "system" and the "chaotic," between tradition and revolution, decadence and vitality, security and danger, reason and imagination. In *Die Hermannsschlacht,* Grabbe once again dramatizes these issues. On the side of the Romans we see the "system" and its decadence. On the side of the Germans, we have primitive vitality and freshness. But the playwright goes beyond the simplified conflict implied by this dualism. Grabbe, as a "historian," shows awareness of the fact that Rome's weakness and strength both lie in the "tradition" and of the fact that the naïve German vitality works both for and against Arminius.

On the one hand, Varus often sounds like Prusias: his literary allusions and schoolmasterly advice on rhetoric suggest a decadent deference to tradition, a blind adherence to forms for their own sake; in short, a confusion of art and life that resembles Prusias' artificiality. On the other hand, we recall Heinrich von Ofterdingen's remark in *Barbarossa*: greatness endures only in the world of poetry. We see in Varus a substantiation of the belief that without literature and the idealism that fosters it, without a feeling for the intangible and imaginative, historical glory cannot exist as a goal. The Germans think only of their own petty problems, and as soon as they have executed the scribes, the automatons, the tangible symbols of their oppression, they are satisfied.

While Varus' constant mention of Horace and other Roman poets may well stem from the vicarious pleasure that produces a love of tradition, we note that the Germans have no poets, no tradition from which they can draw inspiration. We remember Faust's question regarding "world history" as opposed to mere "world events." Varus is aware of the former, but the Germanic tribes know only the latter, that is, the effects, not the causes of actions. Varus' death is almost tragic, because his people, his culture, and his language know world history, and therefore his supposedly ignominious end will be perpetuated. Hermann's victory, however, will have less meaning,

for his claims for historical greatness have been thwarted by
the limitation of the German language and culture. Only the
"event" of the battle will be recalled.

Moreover, if there is truly a "hero" in this play, it is Varus.
Only he undergoes a transformation. At the beginning of the
"First Night," Eggius says about the "bellowing in the mountains," "Our historians and poets call that 'bardiets.'" Varus
answers: "I wish they were sitting here and had to listen to
that bardic yowling in wind and rain" (III, 357). In this
statement, we note not only the transformation of the rather
effete Roman disciple of Horace to an almost cynically realistic
commentator but also the basic conflict in Varus and men like
him. Varus later uses the expression "wheel of history," which
reflects his view of history as overpowering and anonymous, a
force that moves relentlessly without consideration for the
individual. Yet history has meaning only in terms of human
greatness, for the scars on the soldiers' faces are the punctuation
of history's record. Not even Hermann shows such awareness of
the conflict between historical forces and the individual.

Varus worries about what posterity will say about him, for
he realizes that the writers of history do not know about the
events they record. No one will note that he, the realist, saw
the danger of the situation, and that he suffered and died as
a soldier. In his last moment he is no longer a "phrasemaker,"
for he knows that there is nothing else he can say: the wheel
of history has passed over him. The "word," be it historical,
literary, or generally idealistic, has given his life meaning. Yet,
at the end, he realizes the discrepancy between the "word" and
what it purports to describe, between what the historians will
say about him and what he really was. Like Hannibal, he
becomes virtually mute.

Of course, not only Varus but also Hermann is a "phrasemaker." The latter dreams of "Deutschland," but this vision has
been made possible only by his education in the Roman tradition. "Germania" has become "Deutschland," but none of Hermann's compatriots comprehend this concept borrowed from
another language. Hermann's lack of communication with the
Germanic tribes substantiates what the Devil says to Faust:
people can understand only what they can put in words. Since
the Germans do not yet have a word for a union of their tribes,
they cannot have such a union as their goal. Once again the

almighty power of time makes itself felt: Hermann is ahead of his people, for he has a vision for which they are not yet prepared. Varus dies for a dying world. Hermann dreams of a world that cannot be born until the culture of his people permits it.

The conclusion of *Die Hermannsschlacht* offers no hope. As Arthur Kutscher and others have shown, the difference to the superficially similar conclusion of Hebbel's *Herodes und Mariamne* exemplifies how little Grabbe, as conscious as he was of "time," believed in any type of progress. Augustus leaves the stage like an actor who has played out his role, and we are reminded of Grabbe's favorite motif, repeated in some form in almost every play: the world is only a "mediocre comedy." The battle between Varus and Hermann really proved nothing, for the new age is coming from the East. Hebbel's drama intergrates the birth of Christ as the birth of a new love that will replace the barbaric love of Herodes for Mariamne. There is continuity in Hebbel's world, where nothing seems to have existed in vain. In Grabbe's *Hermannsschlacht*, the birth of Christ stresses the fact that the conflict in the North, as far as ideas and principles are concerned, was fought in vain. In Grabbe's world, Henry VI, Sulla, Napoleon, Hannibal, Varus, and Hermann have played their roles, but there is no continuity, for with their deaths they become only memories. None of them have had any permanent effect on the world itself, but only on the imagination of men.

Die Hermannsschlacht is not a good play. Yet its failure cannot be ascribed simply to Grabbe's inability to reveal, once again, an important problem and a meaningful paradox of human existence. In his conception of the issues, as in his formal innovations, Grabbe may well have achieved the dubious honor of having written the best play about Arminius.

CHAPTER 5

Grabbe's Place in
German Literary History

IN the course of our discussion of Grabbe's life and works, we have noted many points of similarity and difference between Grabbe and his contemporaries and predecessors. Such comparisons have, however, illuminated only part of Grabbe's importance in German literary history. The "erring knight of Poetry" from Detmold was convinced that he was writing for the future, and most of us have indeed observed various techniques and themes which strike us as "modern." The overwhelming mass of material determining Grabbe's place in literary history must be drawn, therefore, not from what went on before him, not from what he had in common with his contemporaries, but rather from what was yet to come.

In most respects an iconoclast and revolutionary, Grabbe has, in turn, exercised his greatest attraction on dramatic revolutionaries, who see him as part of a particular tradition of anti-traditionalists in German literature. As far as "modern" drama is concerned, this tradition commences with the *Stürmer und Dränger*, who consciously revolted against the prevalent form of drama in the second half of the eighteenth century. Although Grabbe is in no way just another tardy Storm and Stress poet, he, like Georg Büchner, who tacitly acknowledged his own debt to the Storm and Stress, particularly to Lenz, represents the next step in the genealogy of modern German drama. There exists a lineal development of the modern theater from the *Sturm und Drang*, including Goethe's *Götz von Berlichingen* and Schiller's *Räuber*, through Grabbe and Büchner to Naturalism, Frank Wedekind, Expressionism, Brecht, and the Theater of the Absurd. Another pioneer of Naturalism, Hebbel, could also be mentioned, as could Kleist, on whom the Expressionists and Absurdists were later to draw. But Grabbe and Büchner, who evidence many similarities with Kleist and Hebbel, incor-

154

porate even more qualities in their works that are to be found in the entire spectrum of modern drama. In turn, Grabbe and Büchner in particular had to wait for recognition until those forces that would produce "modern" literature began to materialize.

During the nineteenth century, Grabbe was never completely forgotten, but almost all knowledge of his works was had by reading.[1] During his lifetime, only *Don Juan und Faust* had been performed, and only once each, at that. Subsequently, there were, to be sure, several performances of this work, his only "'drama of ideas' and the play that, in its content and form, most corresponded to post-Romantic mythological dramas like Immermann's *Merlin* and Hebbel's *Gyges und sein Ring*. Grabbe's other, more unconventional dramas experienced a far greater neglect. *Gothland* was first performed in 1892, *Scherz, Satire* in 1876, and not until 1907 did this comedy appear with regularity on the German stage. *Nannette und Maria* has, to Grabbe's good fortune, been produced only twice (1914 and 1922). *Barbarossa* was not performed until 1875 and thereafter only a few times. *Henry VI*, on the other hand, has been somewhat more popular: it was first performed in 1875, two nights after *Barbarossa;* but beginning in 1904 we note several productions in successive years before World War I. The first complete performance of *Napoleon*, which Immermann called Grabbe's best work but never staged, was not until September 2, 1895. And Grabbe's great historical drama, *Hannibal*, was not offered on the stage until 1916, the year in which Expressionists like Reinhard Goering and Walter Hasenclever began writing their pacifist plays. *Die Hermannsschlacht* has been produced only during the Third Reich.

Naturalism, which is generally considered to be the initial phase of modern literature, began in Germany around 1885. As we see, most of the significant productions of Grabbe's works occurred after that date.

I *Grabbe and Naturalism*

To a certain extent, the Naturalists and Grabbe have a common motive in their pursuit of "realism" in an extreme sense. In the first number of *Die Gesellschaft* (Society), dating from January 1, 1885, we read: "Our *Society* aims for the emancipation of the belletristic periodicals and criticism from the tyranny of the 'daughters of good homes' and of the old women of both sexes.... We want to restore to honor the badly endangered masculinity and bravery in knowledge, writing, and criticism. ...We need an organ of whole, free, humane thought, of an undeceived sense of truth, of a resolutely realistic view of the world."

Grabbe called his time a "syrup time," and he laughed at the "herring literature" of his contemporaries, particularly that produced by the women among them. Through his characters he fought the "system" and empty pedantry. Attacking, as he did, the capitulation of the literary world to the banal products of women writers, Grabbe would have understood the attempt by the *Gesellschaft* to restore masculine virtues to literature. In contrast to the saccharine romanticizing of the time, Grabbe demanded a "resolutely realistic view of the world," by implication if not by direct statement. The Naturalists recognized and appeciated Grabbe's propensity toward realism. And from Grabbe's letters and works, we could either infer or establish his agreement with the Naturalists' mission to overturn all empty philistine values.

Moreover, among its accomplishments, Naturalism opened the theatergoing public's eyes to the importance of the mass scenes. Hauptmann's *Die Weber* and *Florian Geyer* let the masses assume the main role, and in the former there is virtually no hero except the collective figure of the weavers. In many other dramas before and after Grabbe there are large masses on the stage, as in Goethe's *Götz,* in Schiller's *Wallenstein,* and in Hebbel's *Agnes Bernauer,* but they remain, by and large, subordinated to a conventional plot development. Hauptmann's *Weber* was one of the first truly "open" dramas to achieve popularity on the stage, and its success stimulated the production of earlier dramas of that type, among them Grabbe's *Napoleon* and Büchner's *Dantons Tod.*

While Grabbe's goal of realism made him particularly attractive to the Naturalists, the reason why he sought a "resolutely realistic view of the world" also characterizes the main difference between him and the doctrinaire Naturalists. The latter proceeded from Zola's *Le roman expérimental* and the doctrine expounded in it. Like the Frenchman, they tried to realize the scientific method in literature. In the German Naturalists' works we find an echo of Zola's famous statement, "L'homme méta-physique est mort, tout notre terrain se transforme avec l'homme physiologique." For Grabbe, man as a "metaphysical being" also no longer exists, for the characters in his drama no longer know whether, or how, they are to be understood metaphysically. But believing, as they do, that science can explain man's situation better than metaphysics, the Naturalists use extreme realism as a testament of belief, not of disbelief. For Grabbe, realism was the only choice left in a world devoid of metaphysical truths.

Thus the realism of the Naturalists reveals itself in a pre-occupation with the minute, the detailed for its own sake. Indeed, Arno Holz and Johannes Schlaf developed a so-called *Sekundenstil*, in which every second of real life is reproduced by a second on the stage. Grabbe, on the other hand, gives us a caricatured world of temporal fragmentation because, in the Nietzschean sense, God must be accepted as dead. The Naturalists saw only a fragmented world, a world of inches and seconds, however, not because they were disillusioned but because everything now seemed measurable. In turn, a measur-able world is a world that can be comprehended. Since man can understand time by measuring the number of seconds, the Naturalist's preoccupation with realistic detail, with a *Sekunden-stil*, no longer symbolizes man's captivity in a godless world, like Gothland's, but rather an affirmation of man's control over it. Ultimately, what Grabbe's attitude toward such a naïve concept of the world would have been is nowhere more evident than in his satire on the scientists in *Scherz, Satire*: even if a radical Naturalist were confronted by the supernatural, he would not believe it, for one can only understand what one can comprehend.

Although Naturalism as a whole contributed markedly to the establishment of a climate in which the plays of Lenz, Grabbe, and Büchner could be reintroduced and appreciated, its greatest playwright, Gerhart Hauptmann, seems to be the exception to the rule that Büchner enthusiasts feel attracted to Grabbe and vice versa. Hauptmann, who read from Büchner's works in the literary club Durch in 1887, took little notice of Grabbe. While no public acknowledgment of an influence by Grabbe on his work was ever made by Hauptmann, we note in Artur Kutscher's biography of Frank Wedekind that Wedekind and Hauptmann, despite their many differences of opinion, often met on common ground in their discussion of Lenz, Grabbe, and Büchner.[2] We may assume with a fair degree of justification, that Hauptmann was not unfavorable in his comments.

II *Grabbe and Wedekind*

Our interest in the further development of German drama forces us to shift our attention, however, from Hauptmann to Wedekind, probably the most salient link between Naturalism and Expressionism and also one of Grabbe's most enthusiastic supporters. In terms of his personality, Wedekind, a notorious rebel against society and its conventions, must have felt drawn to Grabbe. Like him, Wedekind spent most of his life as a literary and social *enfant terrible*, as an Eulenspiegel ridiculing the philistines and as an artist more famous for his experiments than for his accomplishments. Moreover, the most significant experience in his childhood education was his contact with his "philosophical aunt," Olga Plümacher, who was a disciple of Eduard von Hartmann's pessimistic philosophy. Through her Wedekind was introduced, at an early age, to the writers of *Weltschmerz*, among them Grabbe and Büchner.[3] While Wedekind's favorite theme, the erotic drive, is undoubtedly traceable to his youthful preoccupation with Schopenhauer and von Hartmann, his dramatic form stems from an unforgettable contact with Grabbe and Büchner, an influence treated in more detail by Kutscher, Gittleman, and Spalter.

In the theater there is one cardinal sin that no dramatist dare commit: regardless of the import or truth of his "message," he must keep his audience in the theater and awake until the end of his play. In other words, his play must not be boring. It is just such boredom that Wedekind found and criticized in the Naturalist plays. Moreover, he called such theater undemanding on both the actor and the public, mainly because it triggered only the everyday reaction in both. What Wedekind demanded was, in short, the excitement of theater for its own sake.

Moreover, Wedekind's personality was ill-suited for the role of an objective, scientific observer. Although committed to a world of physical and psychological relationships, to a world essentially without God, he shared with the *Weltschmerzler* Heine, Grabbe, and Büchner the "laughter of desperation" about such a world. In short, his drama presents us with people as puppets, puppets as people, people as animals, and animals as people. It is a grotesque world in which the tragic appears comic and vice versa, a carnival—one of his favorite images— in which the characters never talk to one another but only with one another. Wedekind's characters appear, as one critic says, in overdosage (*Überdosierung*), whereby they represent more an inner truth than an external one.

The analogy to Grabbe is obvious. While, for example, the mass scenes in *Napoleon* and *Hannibal* seem almost natural- istically realistic, the many bizarre effects in them reveal that Grabbe is not only copying life but also dramatizing it. More- over, the Prusias scenes in *Hannibal* directly anticipate Wede- kind's style. Prusias is not a parody or satire—or at least only to a very limited and superficial extent. He is an independent character, to be judged only in the context of the drama itself. Like one of Wedekind's characters, he appears in "overdosage"; the world he has created is a world of grotesque marionettes. The same observation could be made of the opening scene in *Napoleon*; the animals, peepshows, reliques of the revolution, and milling crowds for a carnival atmosphere that is strikingly irreal in its grotesqueness, yet undeniably real in its historical import. Many of Grabbe's characters seem to reappear in plays by Wedekind: aside from Count Schneinitz, lifted, as Gittleman says (p. 142) from *Scherz, Satire*, we could also see a close relationship, for example, between Keith, the hero of *Der Marquis von Keith*, and Don Juan or Scholz and Faust. In other words, the combination of realistic caricature and caricatured realism found in Grabbe's works is revived by Wedekind, who thereby bridges the gap between Naturalism and Expressionism.

III   *Grabbe and Expressionism*

If "accuracy" is the goal of the scientifically oriented Natural- ist, "intensity" is the motto of the Expressionist. While the doctrinaire Naturalist includes every banality he might encounter in an actual event, the Expressionist, developing further the objectives of Wedekind, strives for intensity through concen- tration on one aspect, even to the point of caricature and the grotesque. As one of their number says, the "mask" becomes reality. Often the dialogue of Expressionist drama is distilled to ecstatic pathos with virtually no semblance of real conventional language. Speech becomes utterance; syntax is shattered; and the characters function as loudspeakers speaking past one another about ideas. In turn, all contact with the traditional drama of interpersonal relationships is abandoned. Unity becomes a question of themes played by the author, with his characters as instruments.

Much of this technique is already anticipated in the language and structure of *Napoleon* and *Hannibal*, for here and elsewhere Grabbe mixes realism with pathos, diffusion with intense concentration. Not only Grabbe's youthful, "wilder" plays like *Gothland* and *Scherz, Satire*, are structured in an Expressionist manner, but even *Don Juan und Faust*, seemingly more conventional, reveals such techniques. As H.-H. Krummacher has pointed out, the protagonists in *Don Juan und Faust* speak not as individuals but as their "roles" require. We are reminded of Expressionist plays like Sorge's *Bettler*, where the characters appear not as individuals but as types. Moreover, Don Juan and Faust scarcely encounter each other; and when they do, each can express only the idea he symbolizes. The unity of *Don Juan und Faust* rests ultimately on the tragicomic interplay of antithetical ideas rather than on the conflict between two competing lovers. Minor characters like Rubio and Negro appear as grotesque caricatures of social types, and like the Expressionists Grabbe uses them to satirize the banality of conventional society.

In general, Grabbe's less subtle influence on the Expressionists can be seen in his tendency toward shocking effects, obscenity, contempt for middle-class values, and in his seeming glorification of the "superman"—we remember, of course, that Nietzsche, with whom Grabbe has in many points been compared above, was one of the most important influences on the Expressionists. As the *Gefühlsmensch* of German literature Grabbe appears in Hanns Johst's *Der Einsame*, a drama that deals with him with no consideration for biographical fact. And even the "wildest" of Grabbe's dramas, *Gothland*, served Klabund as the basis for a radio play, published in *Sendespiele* III (1926).

IV   *Grabbe in the Third Reich*

If there is a distaste for Grabbe's works today, only a small part of it can be attributed directly to the Expressionist cult.

The greater part can be traced to the "cultural" efforts of the Third Reich. Like Richard Wagner, Grabbe, with far less justification, was transformed by the propaganda machine into a patriotic poet lacking only the brown shirt to be a National Socialist. The new political philosophy claimed—as usual, with little regard for historical fact—to have "discovered" Grabbe, for example, in Alfred Meyer's "Geleitwort" to the *Jahrbuch der Grabbe-Gesellschaft,* I (1939).

Due to the sudden stimulation from the new government, there ensued, of course, many notable productions of Grabbe's works. Several *Grabbe-Wochen* (Grabbe Weeks) were staged, during which *Die Hermannsschlacht* played a dominant role.[4] Paradoxically, the Nazi efforts to revive Grabbe contribute to our better understanding of his work by their failure. Despite the fact that Grabbe was supposed to be a *völkischer Dichter* (people's poet) and an exponent of the "Führer principle," we find that only few of his works justify such a description—if any at all. Most often performed was the *Hermannsschlacht,* mainly because it seemed to sound the call for German unity under a strong, "visionary" leader. Yet the really memorable productions were not of this drama or any other with a German setting, but rather of *Don Juan und Faust* and *Napoleon,* in both of which the specifically German element seems of questionable value; for example, Gustav Gründgens starred as Don Juan in 1936, and this role appears to have pleased him so much that he celebrated his twenty-fifth anniversary as *Intendant* by producing the play again.

V   *Grabbe and Brecht*

In his "Anmerkungen zur Oper *Aufstieg und Fall der Stadt Mahagonny*" and elsewhere, Brecht claims that "the modern theater is the epic theater." In essence, Brecht sets up a strawman, which he calls "Aristotelian" drama. He then proceeds to knock over this strawman with his "epic" criteria. Unfortunately, the limits of space prohibit our discussing in detail how Brecht mixes esthetic and social elements in his definition of the "epic." (For example, Brecht himself once said that the "epic" is "a category of the social and not of the esthetic-formal.")

Nevertheless, Brecht contributed a great deal to our understanding and appreciation of the epic, undramatic tendencies of modern drama. Since the end of World War II, more and more attention has been directed toward his new conception of drama, and in turn several critics—most prominent among them Spalter—have commented directly and indirectly on Grabbe's role in the evolution of the "epic theater" as genre.

In Grabbe's time, "epic" aspects of any drama were grounds for rejection. One of the most famous criticisms leveled against Grabbe's works stems from Heinrich Laube, the director of the Vienna Burgtheater from 1849 to 1867. He was certainly not insensitive to dramatic ability which had escaped the less astute public, for it was he who rediscovered Grillparzer for the stage. Yet in speaking about Grabbe's *Hohenstaufen,* Laube says, "I learned that Grabbe does not write dramatically; he only describes dramatically. That, on the stage, is sure death."[5] If this almost aphoristic judgment does indeed have any substance, it is that Grabbe appears to have interpolated the characters as narrators of the happenings. In other words, there seems to be an epic mediation between the audience and the events. But one of Brecht's most important criteria is the narration of the action rather than its being acted out. In other words, Brecht affirms the very technique criticized by Laube.

Moreover, since Brecht was himself highly indebted to the innovations of the Expressionists, much of his theory, which they anticipated, had already been realized by Grabbe. For example, Brecht calls for a "montage" and "each scene for itself," a technique common to most of Grabbe's works. According to Brecht, the plot should develop "in curves" instead of "linearly." This requirement is satisfied by almost all of Grabbe's works. In other words, Grabbe occupies a prominent position in the lineage of Brecht's "epic" theater, not only as the product of one man, but also as a general phenomenon of the modern stage.

VI *Grabbe and the Theater of the Absurd*

In terms of the underlying ideas and conception of existence in Grabbe's plays, he looms as a pioneer of the Theater of the Absurd. In *The Theater of the Absurd,*[6] an excellent study of this development, Martin Esslin shows that the Absurdists, like any group, have clearly discernible predecessors, among them Grabbe. He cites the translation of *Scherz, Satire,* which he calls a "masterpiece of *humour noire*," by Alfred Jarry, an important forerunner of the Absurdists. Recounting the heritage of the movement, Esslin says that the line of development leads directly from Grabbe and Büchner to Wedekind, the Dadaists, German Expressionism, and the early Brecht (p. 240). But Esslin, while making a valuable contribution to the subject, nevertheless leaves much unsaid.

For example, Grabbe's Prusias, as well as all of the characters that resemble him in varying degrees, seem to correspond to Esslin's description of Absurdist characterization (pp. 300f.): the motives and actions of the characters appear largely incomprehensible to the audience, who in turn cannot identify with these characters; because they evoke no identification, the Absurdist characters seem comic, yet the subject matter of this comic theater is somber, violent, and bitter; the result is the dominance of tragicomedy in the Theater of the Absurd. Not only Prusias, but almost all of the persons in *Scherz, Satire*, in Esslin's sense of the word, "transcend" in like manner the comic and tragic.[7]

In its basic tenet, in its concept of human existence as "absurd," the Theater of the Absurd echoes Grabbe's own view of life. In the *Myth of Sisyphus*, Albert Camus states the case of the Absurdists of his generation: "A world that can be explained by reasoning, however faulty, is a familiar world. But in a universe that is suddenly deprived of illusions and of light, man feels a stranger.... This divorce between man and his life, the actor and his setting, truly constitutes the feeling of Absurdity" (quoted by Esslin, p. xix). This statement does, indeed, seem to be a resignation to nihilism and could be associated with many disillusioned poets of the nineteenth century, especially with the *Weltschmerzler*. Camus asserts that reason is all that man has, yet his reason can provide no answers to the meaning of existence. Because this attitude pervades so much of *Weltschmerz*, a renaissance of Grabbe, Büchner, Heine, and other kindred spirits was not long in coming.

Yet the Absurdists reject not only reason as an abstract concept. They renounce the main instrument with which man reasons, language, as well. One clearly discernible link between Grabbe and the Absurdists is the prominent role of langauge as a motif in their works and their mutual rejection of "words."

In his discussion of Ionesco's *La Cantatrice Chauve*, Esslin reports the following: "Ionesco read his play to a group of friends. They found it funny, although *he* believed himself to have written a very serious piece, 'the tragedy of language'" (p. 88). And we recall that Faust's tragedy arose, in Grabbe's version, from his expression of the wish in the subjunctive: to learn how he could have found tranquillity and happiness. The fulfillment of his wish can never be experienced but only stated. Furthermore, Faust can never find the ultimate meaning of the universe because he, like all men, cannot transcend the barrier of language. "Words" are, for all of Grabbe's characters, only a part of a "mediocre comedy."

The result of the Absurdists' rejection of language is their reliance on, as Esslin says, "pure" theater (p. 230). Pure theater is the theater of gesture, of the *commedia dell'arte*, which was also one of the inspirations for Tieck's fantastic comedies and indirectly for Grabbe. We recall the many absurd gestures in Grabbe's dramas: for example, the unmotivated murder of thirteen tailors in *Scherz, Satire* could have been lifted out of an Absurdist drama. And one of the most absurd, grotesque gestures in German literature is that of Prusias at the conclusion of *Hannibal.* Nor may we ignore the most monumental "gesture": the battle. The battle functions in Grabbe's dramas like the senseless actions of the Theater of the Absurd. To be sure, the battles seem to be intelligible. Only in retrospect do we realize that, as in the Absurd, "the relevant question [is] not so much what is going to happen next but what is happening" (Esslin, p. 305). In *Napoleon, Hannibal,* and *Die Hermannsschlacht* the battles are the sole judgment of the heroes' actions, but they lead to nothing and are, for that reason, absurd.

It is obvious that Grabbe anticipated many of the techniques that came to characterize modern drama and that his underlying view of existence is no less modern than that of the Absurdists. And perhaps new developments in the theater of tomorrow will call attention to additional aspects in which it was anticipated by Christian Dietrich Grabbe.

Notes and References

Chapter One

1. *Memorabilien, Zweiter Teil,* in: *Schriften* (Hamburg: Hoffmann und Campe, 1843), XI, 2nd part, p. 61.

2. The lively interest in Grabbe's personal life can, in no small measure, be attributed to the controversy that soon raged about the first biography, Eduard Duller's *Grabbe,* which appeared as the introduction to *Die Hermannsschlacht* (Düsseldorf: J. H. C. Schreiner, 1838). Duller's work, based on the information supplied by Grabbe's wife, is far from impartial or free from distortion. The next important biographical attempt, which arose from the author's wish to correct the misinformation in Duller's biography, is Carl Georg Heinrich Ziegler's *Grabbe's [sic] Leben und Charakter* (Hamburg: Hoffmann und Campe, 1855). But Ziegler too patently shows the desire of a friend to save Grabbe's and his mother's image. Grabbe's definitive biography is yet to be written. The best evaluation of all the known evidence about Grabbe and of the above biographies can be found in Alfred Bergmann, *Die Glaubwürdigkeit der Zeugnisse für den Lebensgang und Charakter Christian Dietrich Grabbes,* Germanische Studien, No. 137 (Berlin: Ebering, 1933). Bergmann, without doubt the greatest living expert on Grabbe, later edited *Grabbe in Berichten seiner Zeitgenossen* (Stuttgart: Metzler, 1968), which complements his study of 1933. The reader is, however, also referred to the biographical material in the books by F. J. Schneider and R. A. Nicholls, both listed in the Selected Bibliography.

3. See for example, Herbert Eulenberg's image of Grabbe in *Neue Bilder* (Berlin: Bruno Cassirer, 1918), 17th ed.

4. See Alfred Bergmann, *Das Detmolder Zuchthaus als Stätte von Christian Dietrich Grabbes Kindheit und Jugend. Jahresgabe der Grabbe-Gesellschaft 1967/68* (Detmold, 1968), for all available information on Grabbe's years in this environment.

5. Interestingly enough, the first American book-length study on Grabbe was Horace Lind Hoch's *Shakespeare's Influence upon Grabbe* ([Philadelphia, 1911]), originally a dissertation at the University of Pennsylvania. Some of Lind's comparisons are, however, somewhat strained, and although several essays on this subject have appeared in the meantime, much work remains to be done.

6. *Sämtliche Werke,* ed. Ernst Elster (Leipzig: Bibliographisches Institut [1897]), VII, 469.

7. There is, however, a well-known but probably apocryphal anecdote that Grabbe once administered the oath to two witnesses in his office while he was wearing an officer's hat, service jacket, underwear, stockings, and slippers—and one of the witnesses was a woman. See Bergmann, *Grabbe in Berichten,* p. 83.

8. All contemporary criticism of his works has been collected by Alfred Bergmann in *Grabbes Werke in der zeitgenössischen Kritik* (Detmold: Grabbe-Gesellschaft, 1958ff.), which has appeared in six volumes as *Jahresgaben der Grabbe-Gesellschaft.*

Chapter Two

1. We are struck by divine overtones in the King, who is, in essence, an antipode of the satanic Berdoa. See my article on "Satan and the Satanic in Grabbe's Dramas," *Germanic Review,* XXXIX (1964), 120-36.

2. Grabbe later made the same remark about the Devil (V, 316) and has it substantiated by the Knight (Devil) in *Don Juan und Faust.*

3. Cited by R. A. Nicholls in his excellent interpretation of *Scherz, Satire.*

4. Here Grabbe is also attacking the often unrestrained "Calderón-mania" of the Romantics, a target of many other post-Romantic writers, for example, Franz Grillparzer.

5. Cf. Jürgen Schröder, *Georg Büchners "Leonce und Lena": Eine verkehrte Komödie* (Munich: Fink, 1966).

6. Karl S. Guthke (*op. cit.,* p. 197) denies *Scherz, Satire* tragicomic stature. He is correct only in as far as *Scherz, Satire* alone is concerned, but, taken together with *Gothland,* it provides half of a tragicomic illumination of the same set of problems. Guthke, seemingly aware of such an approach, denies the close relationship of the two plays (footnote 48, p. 416), a contention the following parallels will refute.

7. R. A. Nicholls, however, points out several advantages of the first version over the second.

Chapter Three

1. Peter Michelsen, "Verführer und Übermensch: Zu Grabbes 'Don Juan und Faust,'" *Jahrbuch der Raabe-Gesellschaft* (1965), 83, emphasizes that the popularity of the Faust-figure coincides with the rise of the bourgeoisie.

2. On the sources of *Aschenbrödel* see the "Nachwort" to: *Aschenbrödel,* ed. Alfred Bergmann, Jahresgabe der Grabbe-Gesellschaft 1949/50 (Detmold: Grabbe-Gesellschaft, 1950), pp. 113-60. A brief account is available in English in R. A. Nicholl's chapter on this comedy.

Chapter Four

1. The most complete and reliable account of Grabbe's sources for *Napoleon* is provided by Alfred Bergmann, *Quellen des Grabbeschen "Napoleon," Jahresgabe der Grabbe-Gesellschaft* 1969 (Detmold: Grabbe-Gesellschaft, 1969), which not only corrects misconceptions in previous works but also provides invaluable new information.

Chapter Five

1. In *Daş Grabbe-Buch,* ed. Paul Friedrich and Fritz Ebers (Detmold: Meyer, 1923), Alfred Bergmann presents a list of Grabbe productions before 1923.

2. *Frank Wedekind. Sein Leben und seine Werke* (Munich: Georg Müller, 1922), I, 177.

3. See Sol Gittleman, *Frank Wedekind,* Twayne's World Authors Series, No. 55 (New York: Twayne, 1969), p. 8.

4. See *Christian Dietrich Grabbe: Die Grabbewoche 1936 im Urteil der Deutschen Presse,* ed. Heinrich Hollo (Detmold: NS.-Verlag, 1936), pp. 41-44. Although a part of Grabbe's sudden popularity might be attributed to the fact that Hanns Johst had become president of the Reichsschrifttumskammer, the Nazi organization for writers, the image of Grabbe promoted by the government was not that of the ecstatic poet.

5. *Heinrich Laubes gesammelte Werke in fünfzig Bänden,* ed. Heinrich Hubert Houben (Leipzig, 1909), XXXII, 113. Note also Grabbe's remark on *Napoleon*: "We have earned making a dramatic-epic revolution and good fortune with *Napoleon*" (VI, 18).

6. Anchor Books, No. 279 (New York: Doubleday, 1961).

7. See also Nicholls' interpretation of the farcical in *Scherz, Satire.*

Chapter Four

1. The most complete and reliable account of Origen sources...

Chapter Three

1. ...
2. ...
3. ...

Selected Bibliography

PRIMARY SOURCES

Christian Dietrich Grabbe: *Werke*, ed. Alfred Bergmann (Emsdetten: Lechte Verlag, 1960ff.). The four volumes containing Grabbe's works have already appeared; until the publication of the last two volumes, the letters must be cited from the following edition: *Grabbes Werke*, ed. Spiridion Wukadinowić (Berlin: Bong [1912]). The only edition for English-speaking students is *Scherz, Satire, Ironie und tiefere Bedeutung*, ed. Roy C. Cowen (Waltham: Blaisdell, 1969). A translation of "Jest, Satire, Irony and Deeper Significance" appears in: Eric Bentley, *From the Modern Repertoire, Series Two* (Bloomington: Indiana University Press, 1952). The only other play that has been completely translated is "Don Juan and Faust" in: *The Theater of Don Juan*, ed. Oscar Mandel (Lincoln: University of Nebraska Press, 1963). Max Spalter (see below) also offers a translation of *Napoleon*, Act I, scene 1 and Act III, scene 1.

SECONDARY SOURCES

The reader is referred to the biographical material cited in the footnotes to Chapter One. An asterisk denotes studies referred to in the text.

BERGMANN, ALFRED. "Grabbeforschung und Grabbeprobleme 1918-1934," *Germanisch-Romanische Monatsschrift*, 22 (1934), 343-57, 437-57.

————. *Die Vorfahren Grabbes* (Detmold: Meyer, 1937).

————. *Meine Grabbesammlung* (Detmold: Schnelle, 1942).

————. *Die historisch-kritische Ausgabe von Grabbes Werken und Briefwechsel. Jahresgabe der Grabbe-Gesellschaft 1950/51* (Detmold: Grabbe-Gesellschaft, 1951).

————. *Grabbe als Benutzer der öffentlichen Bibliothek in Detmold* (Detmold: Private Printing, 1965).

BÖTTGER, FRITZ. *Grabbe. Glanz und Elend eines Dichters* (Berlin: Verlag der Nation [1963]). A Marxist interpretation.

BUSCH, ERNST. "Geschichte und Tragik in Grabbes Dramen," *Dichtung und Volkstum*, 41 (1941), 440-59.

COWEN, ROY C. "Satan and the Satanic in Grabbe's Dramas," *Germanic Review*, 39 (1964), 120-36.

169

————. "Grabbe's *Don Juan und Faust* and Büchner's *Dantons Tod:* Epicureanism and *Weltschmerz,*" *Publications of the Modern Language Association,* 82 (1967), 342-51.

————. "Grabbe's Napoleon, Büchner's Danton, and the Masses," *Symposium,* 21 (1967), 316-23.

DIEKMANN, ERNST. *Christian Dietrich Grabbe: Der Wesensgehalt seiner Dichtung* (Detmold: Meyer, 1936).

EBERT, BERNHARD. "Grabbe als Jurist," *Mitteilungen aus der lippischen Geschichte und Landeskunde,* 20 (1951), also as special printing of two hundred copies for the Grabbe-Gesellschaft; 37 pp.

FRIEDRICH, PAUL and EBERS, FRITZ, ed. *Das Grabbe-Buch* (Detmold: Meyer, 1923). Essays on Grabbe, Schopenhauer, Nietzsche, Müllner, Immermann, and Hebbel; a list of performances and a bibliography compiled by Alfred Bergmann; miscellaneous material.

GERRESHEIM, HELGA-MALEEN. "Christian Dietrich Grabbe," in: *Deutsche Dichter des 19. Jahrhunderts, Ihr Leben und Werk,* ed. Benno von Wiese (Berlin: Erich Schmidt, 1969).

GREINER, MARTIN. *Zwischen Biedermeier und Bourgeoisie* (Göttingen: Vandenhoeck & Ruprecht, 1953), pp. 181-218 (originally published in Leipzig).

°GUTHKE, KARL S. *Geschichte und Poetik der deutschen Tragikomödie* (Göttingen: Vandenhoeck & Ruprecht, 1961), pp. 197-207.

°HEGELE, WOLFGANG. *Grabbes Dramenform,* Zur Erkenntnis der Dichtung, No. 7 (Munich: Fink, 1970).

KAUFMANN, FRIEDRICH WILHELM. "Die realistische Tendenz in Grabbes Dramen," *Smith College Studies in Modern Languages,* No. 12 (1931), 1-47. An English version appears in the author's *German Dramatists of the 19th Century* (Los Angeles: Lymanhouse, 1940).

KOCH, FRANZ. "Grabbe und Büchner," in: *Idee und Wirklichkeit* (Düsseldorf: Ehlermann, 1956), II, 1-28.

°KRUMMACHER, HANS-HENRIK. "Bemerkungen zur dramatischen Sprache in Grabbes *Don Juan und Faust,*" in: *Festgabe für Eduard Berend,* ed. Hans Werner Seiffert and Bernhard Zeller (Weimar: Böhlau, 1959), pp. 235-56.

°KUEHNEMUND, RICHARD. *Arminius or the Rise of a National Symbol (From Hutten to Grabbe),* University of North Carolina Studies in the Germanic Languages and Literatures, Vol. 8 (Chapel Hill: North Carolina University Press, 1953).

°KUTSCHER, ARTUR. *Hebbel und Grabbe* (Munich: Bachmair, 1913).

MARTINI, FRITZ. "Grabbes niederdeutsches Drama," *Germanisch-Romanische Monatsschrift,* 30 (1942), 87-106, 153-71.

————. "Napoleon oder die Hundert Tage," in: *Das deutsche Drama*, ed. Benno von Wiese (Düsseldorf: Bagel, 1958), II, 43-64.

*NICHOLLS, ROGER. *The Dramas of Christian Dietrich Grabbe*, Studies in German Literature, Vol. 12 (The Hague: Mouton, 1969). Includes, in slightly modified form, the author's previous articles on Grabbe's comedies and on the *Hohenstaufen*.

NIESCHMIDT, HANS-WERNER. *Christian Dietrich Grabbe. Zwei Studien* (Detmold: Schnelle, 1951). Studies on Byron's influence on *Don Juan und Faust* and on the structure of *Hannibal*.

*NIETEN, OTTO. *Christian Dietrich Grabbe: Sein Leben und seine Werke*, Schriften der Literarhistorischen Gesellschaft Bonn, No. 4 (Dortmund: Ruhfus, 1908).

*PIPER, CARL ANTON. *Beiträge zum Studium Grabbes*, Forschungen zur neueren Litteraturgeschichte, No. 8 (Munich: Haushalter, 1898). Studies on "Grabbe, eine psychopathische Erscheinung," pp. 1-50 and "Herzog Theodor von Gothland," pp. 51-145.

*SCHNEIDER, FERDINAND JOSEF. "Das tragische Faustproblem in Grabbes *Don Juan und Faust*," *Deutsche Vierteljahrschrift für Literaturwissenschaft und Geistesgeschichte*, 8 (1930), 539-57.

————. "Christian Dietrich Grabbe und der jungdeutsche Liberalismus," *Euphorion*, 32 (1931), 165-79.

*————. *Christian Dietrich Grabbe. Persönlichkeit und Werk* (Munich: Beck, 1934).

SENGLE, FRIEDRICH. *Das deutsche Geschichtsdrama* (Stuttgart: Metzler, 1952), pp. 121-32.

*SIEBURG, FRIEDRICH. *Christian Dietrich Grabbe: Napoleon oder die hundert Tage*, Dichtung und Wirklichkeit, No. 4 (Berlin: Ullstein, 1963).

SIEFERT, FRITZ. *Christian Dietrich Grabbes Geschichtsdramen* (Bad Godesberg: Private Printing, 1957).

*SPALTER, MAX. *Brecht's Tradition* (Baltimore: The Johns Hopkins Press, 1967), pp. 39-74, 215-35.

*WIESE, BENNO VON. *Die deutsche Tragödie von Lessing bis Hebbel*, 3rd edition (Hamburg: Hoffmann & Campe, 1955), pp. 470-530.

*————. "Grabbes Lustspiel *Scherz, Satire, Ironie und tiefere Bedeutung* als Vorform des absurden Theaters" and "Die Deutung der Geschichte durch den Dramatiker Grabbe" in: *Von Lessing bis Grabbe: Studien zur deutschen Klassik und Romantik* (Düsseldorf: Bagel, 1968), pp. 289-309 and 309-29.

*WEISS, WALTER. *Enttäuschter Pantheismus*, Gesetz und Wandel, Innsbrucker Literarhistorische Arbeiten, No. 3 (Dornbirn: Vorarlberger Verlagsanstalt, 1962), pp. 121-248.

Index

173